SPEAK MANDARIN CHINESE WITH CONFIDENCE

ESSENTIAL MANDARIN CHINESE
PHRASEBOOK & DICTIONARY

Hi, How are you?
Nǐ hǎo ma?

Where are you from?
Nǐ shì nǎguórén?

I'm an American.
Wǒ shì Měiguórén.

Catherine Dai

TUTTLE Publishing

Tokyo | Rutland, Vermont | Singapore

Contents

Introduction

Welcome to the Tuttle Essential Language series, covering all of the most popular Asian languages. These books are basic guides to communicating in the language. They're concise, accessible and easy to understand, and you'll find them indispensable on your trip abroad to get you where you want to go, pay the right prices and do everything you're planning to do.

Each guide is divided into 14 themed sections and starts with a pronunciation guide which explains the phonetic pronunciations of all the words and sentences you'll need to know, and a basic grammar guide which will help you construct basic sentences in the language. At the end of this book is an extensive English–Mandarin Chinese dictionary.

Throughout the book you'll come across boxes with a beside them. These are designed to help you if you can't understand what your listener is saying to you. Hand the book over to them and encourage them to point to the appropriate answer to the question you are asking.

Other boxes in the book—this time without the symbol—give listings of themed words with their English translations beside them.

For extra clarity, we have put all phonetic pronunciations of the Mandarin Chinese terms in bold.

This book covers all situations you are likely to encounter during the course of a visit, from reserving a room for the night to ordering food and drinks at a restaurant and what to do if you get lost or you lose your money. With over 2,000 commonly used words and essential sentences at your fingertips you can rest assured that you will be able to get by in all situations, so let **Essential Mandarin Chinese** become your passport to learning to communicate with confidence!

Pronunciation guide

The book uses the standard romanized system of Mandarin Chinese called Hanyu Pinyin.

Consonants

Most of the Chinese consonants are similar to the English ones, with the following exceptions:

Pinyin	Pronunciation	Example
c	like **ts** in i**ts**	粗 **cū** "rough"
q	like **ch** in **ch**eer, with a strong puff of air	去 **qù** "go"
x	likc **sh** in **sh**e	西 **xī** "west"
z	like **ds** in ki**ds**	字 **zì** "word"
zh	like **dg** as in ju**dg**e, with the tongue rolled back	这 **zhè** "this"

Vowels

Most of the Chinese vowels are similar to English also:

Pinyin	Pronunciation	Example
a	short **a**, as in f**a**r	八 **bā** "eight"
e	short **e**, as in th**e**	鹅 **é** "goose"
i	long **ee**, as in f**ee**	七 **qī** "seven"
o	short **o**, as in f**o**r	我 **wǒ** "I, me"
u	long **u**, as in c**u**te	哭 **kū** "cry"
ü	as in **yü** or the French **u**	绿 **lǜ** "green"

Combination Vowels

The combination vowels are also fairly similar to those in English:

Pinyin	Pronunciation	Example
ao	like **ow** in n**ow**	好 **hǎo** "good"
ei	like **ay** in s**ay**	黑 **hēi** "black"
er	like **er** in numb**er**, with a longer "r" sound	二 **èr** "two"
ian	like **yen**	天 **tiān** "sky"
ie	like **ea** in w**ea**r	鞋 **xié** "shoe"
iu	like **ew** as in p**ew**	丢 **diū** "throw"
ou	like **ow** in l**ow**	猴 **hǒu** "monkey"
ui	like **way** in s**way**	水 **shuǐ** "water"
uo	like **wo** in s**wo**rd	说 **shuō** "word"
ue	like **ue** in fl**ue**nt	学 **xuě** "study"

Tones

A tone is a variation in pitch when a syllable or word is pronounced. In Mandarin, a variation in the pitch or tone changes the meaning of the word. Mandarin has four different tones, each marked by a sign above the vowel. In addition there is a neutral tone which does not carry any mark—often used in the second syllable of a word, e.g., **nǐmen** 你们 "you" (plural). Below is a tone chart which shows how the tones work.

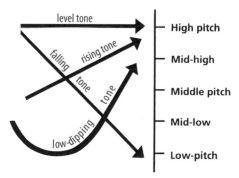

Tone 1 is a high-level tone represented by a level tone mark ▬ above the vowel.

Tone 2 is a high-rising tone represented by a rising tone mark ╱ above the vowel.

Tone 3 is a low-dipping tone represented by a dish-like concave tone mark ╲╱ above the vowel.

Tone 4 is a high-falling tone represented by a falling tone mark ╲ above the vowel.

The neutral tone is pronounced lightly and softly in comparison to the other tones and is not marked by any tone symbol. A syllable is said to take on a neutral tone when it is not emphasized or stressed in the sentence, (i.e., it is skipped over quickly).

Take care to pronounce the words accurately according to their tone marks, as the same syllable can have several different meanings. For example,

Word	Tone Number	Meaning
妈 mā	1	mother
麻 má	2	numb
马 mǎ	3	horse
骂 mà	4	scold
吗 ma	neutral tone	question marker

Pronouncing a word with a different tone can change its meaning. For example, "I'm looking for my mother" can become "I'm looking for my horse"!

Basic grammar

Chinese grammar is very simple. There are no verb conjugations, no plurals, no gender forms, no articles and the sentence order is essentially the same as English. This section presents a basic guide to Chinese grammar in terms familiar to English speakers.

1 Word order

Chinese word order is the same as in English: **subject + verb + object**.

> **Wǒ bú huì shuō Hànyǔ.**
> *I   not can   speak   Chinese* = I don't speak Chinese.

> **Wǒ yào qù Běijīng.**
> *I   want go   Beijing* = I want to go to Beijing.

> **Qǐng gěi wǒ yí bēi lěng kāishuǐ.**
> *Please give me one glass cold   drinking water*
> = I'd like a glass of cold water.

When asking a question, add the question word **ma** 吗 at the end of the sentence. (See page 13)

> **Nǐ huì shuō Hànyǔ   ma?**
> *You can speak Chinese* (question marker)
> = Do you speak Chinese?

> **Nǐ yào qù Běijīng   ma?**
> *You want go   Beijing* (question marker)
> = Do you want to go to Beijing?

> **Nǐ kěyí gěi wǒ yí bēi lěng kāi shuǐ   ma?**
> *You can   give me one glass cold water* (question marker)
> = Can you give me a glass of cold (drinking)water?

2 Nouns

Mandarin nouns often consist of two characters or syllables joined together. For example, **Hànyǔ** "the Chinese language",

lǎoshī "teacher" or **kāfēi** "coffee". No distinction is made between the singular and plural forms. When it is necessary to indicate a plural, this is done by adding a number and a measure word to indicate the number of items involved (see page 10).

3 Pronouns

Chinese pronouns are used just as we use English pronouns. The same word can have two meanings, for example, **wǒ** 我 can refer to both "I" and "me". The other pronouns in Chinese are **nǐ** 你 "you", **tā** 他 "he/him", **tā** 她 "she/her" and **tā** 它 "it" (the last three all share the same pronunciation but are written with different characters).

To indicate plural forms, you add the suffix **-men** 们 so the plural forms are **wǒmen** 我们 "we/us", **nǐmen** 你们 "you" (plural), **tāmen** 他们 "they/them" (either all male or mixed genders) and **tāmen** 她们 "they/them" (all female). The pronoun for animals or insects is **tāmen** 它们 "they/them" (same pronunciation but different characters).

4 "This" and "That"

In addition to the personal pronouns, there are demonstrative pronouns **zhè** 这 "this" and **nà** 那 "that". The plural forms are: **zhè xiē** 这些 "these" and **nà xiē** 那些 "those".

5 Possessives

To indicate possession, simply add the particle **de** 的 between the words. Thus,

Wǒ   **de**   **shu**
I/me (possessive particle) *book* = "my book"

Nǐ   **de**   **shǒujī**
You (possessive particle) *mobile phone*
= "your mobile phone"

Jīntiān   **de**   **tiānqì**   **zěnmeyàng?**
Today (possessive particle) *weather* *what's like*
= What's the weather going to be like today?

Wǒ shuō   **de**   **huà**
I speak (possessive particle) *words* = "the words I'm saying"

Nǐmen	**de**	**diànnǎo**
you (plural form)	(possessive particle)	*laptop* (or computer)

= "your laptop"

6 Measure Words

Just as we would say "two cups of coffee" in English, in Chinese, the number comes first, followed by a measure word like **zhāng** 张 "sheet" and **běn** 本 "measure word for books" and finally, the object **zhǐ** 纸 "paper" or **shū** 书 "books".

yī	**zhāng**	**zhǐ**
one	*sheet*	*paper* = "one sheet of paper"

liǎng	**bēi**	**kāfēi**
two	*cups*	*coffee* = "two cups of coffee"

sān	**běn**	**shū**
three	(measure word for books)	*books* = "three books"

Take note that when counting objects, the word for **èr** 二 "two" becomes **liǎng** 两 "a couple of". Here are some common measure words.

Measure words	Used for	Examples
zhāng 张	flat, wide objects	**yì zhāng zhǐ** "one sheet of paper" **yì zhāng zhuōzi** "one table"
běn 本	bound books	**sān běn shū** "three books"
zhī 只	one out of a pair	**yì zhī shǒu** "one hand"
zhī 支	stick-like objects	**liǎng zhī bǐ** "two pens"
liàng 辆	vehicles with wheels	**sān liàng chē** "three cars"
shuāng 双	a pair	**yì shuāng xié** "a pair of shoes"
tiáo 条	long pieces of clothing or fabric and roads	**liǎng tiáo kùzi** "two (pairs of) pants"
bēi 杯	cups or glasses	**liǎng bēi kāfēi** "two cups of coffee"

If you can't remember all these, there is an all-purpose measure word **ge** 个 which can be used instead of the above measure words **yī ge shū** "one book" or **sì ge xíngli** "four suitcases".

The word **ge** 个 means "piece" and is also used in phrases like **zhè ge** 这个 "this one", **nà ge** 那个 "that one", **nǎ ge** 哪个 "which one" or **jǐ ge** 几个 "how many (items)?"

7 Verbs

Chinese verbs are never conjugated, and have only one simple form regardless of subject or tense. Thus the verb **chī** "to eat" is the same whether the subject is I, you, he/she or they, and whether the action took place in the past, present or future. For example,

Wǒ chī jiǎozi.
I eat dumplings = "I eat dumplings."

This sentence can mean "I ate dumplings" or "I am eating dumplings".

Wǒ qù Běijīng.
I go Beijing = "I am going to Beijing."

Similarly, this could mean "I went to Beijing", "I am going to Beijing" or "I will go to Beijing".

8 Past and future tense

To indicate time in Chinese, you add in time words like "yesterday", "today", "tomorrow", "already" and "will". For example:

Wǒ zuótiān chī jiǎozi.
I yesterday eat dumplings = "Yesterday I ate dumplings."

Wǒ jīntiān chī jiǎozi.
I today eat dumplings = "Today I am eating dumplings."

Wǒ míngtiān chī jiǎozi.
I tomorrow eat dumplings. = "Tomorrow I'll eat dumplings."

You can also add the following to indicate time:

- The addition of **guo** 过="passed" after the verb indicates that the action occurred at an unspecified time in the past:

Wǒ chī guo jiǎozi.
I ate (passed) dumplings = "I've eaten dumplings already."

- The use of **le** 了="completed" after the verb indicates actions that were just completed:

Wǒ chī le jiǎozi.
I ate (completed) dumplings = "I've just eaten dumplings."

- The addition of **yào** 要="want" or **huì** 会 = "will/shall" before the verb indicates a future action:

Wǒ yào chī jiǎozi.
I want eat dumplings = "I'm going to eat the dumplings."

Wǒ huì chī nàxiē jiǎozi.
I will eat those dumplings
= "I'll be eating those dumplings."

9 Adjectives

Adjectives generally precede the nouns they modify, sometimes with the possessive word **de** 的 added in between. For example,

xiǎo xióngmāo	"a small panda"
zāng yīfu	"dirty clothes"
hǎo péngyou	"good friends"
měilì de fēngjǐng	"beautiful scenery"
míngguì de lǐwù	"expensive gift"
tǎoyàn de wénzi	"annoying mosquitoes"

10 Adverbs

Adverbs are usually placed before the words they modify. Common examples are: **hěn** 很 "very", **yě** 也 "also", **bǐjiào** 比较 "comparatively, relatively", **jiù** 就 "then", **zǒng** 总 "always". For example,

Chángchéng hěn cháng.
Great Wall very long = "The Great Wall is very long."

Wǒ yě xiǎng qù Shànghǎi.
I also want go Shanghai = "I want to go to Shanghai too."

Shànghǎi xiàtiān bǐjiào rè.
Shanghai summer rather hot
= "Shanghai is rather hot in summer."

Nǐ xiān zǒu, wǒ mǎshàng jiù lái
You first go, I immediately then come
= "Go first, I'll join you very soon."

Wǔyuè de shíhou, zhè lǐ zǒng xiàyǔ.
May (month) (possessive) *time this place always rains*
= "In May, it always rains here."

11 Negatives

There are two common words used to express the negative in Chinese: **bù** 不 and **méi** 没. The most often used one is **bù** 不 = "not". The word **méi** 没 is used express actions not completed as in 没有 **měiyǒu** = "do not have", "did not".

Fàncài bù hǎo chī.
Food not good eat — "The food is not good."

Wǒ bù qù le.
I not go anymore = "I am not going anymore."

Tā bù zài zhèr.
He not at here = "He's not here."

Wǒ zhǎo bù dào zhège dìzhǐ.
I find cannot this address = "I cannot find this address."

12 Questions

There are three ways to ask a question in Chinese. The easiest way is to add the word **ma** 吗 at the end of the sentence. This word functions like a question mark.

Nǐ huì shuō Yīngyǔ ma?
You can speak English (question marker)
= "Can you speak English?"

Nǐ shì Bǐdé ma?
You are Peter (question marker) = "Are you Peter?"

The second way is to use the yes/no verbal construction which presents two opposing alternatives.

Nǐ huì bu huì shuō Yīngyǔ?
You can not can speak English = "Can you speak English?"

Nǐ shì bu shì Bǐdé?
You are not are Peter = "Are you Peter?"

The third way is to use a question word like **shéi** "who", **shénme** "what", **nǎli/nǎr** "where", **wèishénme** "why", **jǐ** "how many", **nǎ** "which" and **zěnme** "how". Here are some examples of questions you can ask.

1. **Nǐ shì shéi/shuí?**
   You are who = "Who are you?"

2. **Nǐ jiào shénme míngzi?**
   You called what name = "What's your name?"

3. **Nǐ zěnme qù jīcháng?**
   You how go airport = "How are you going to the airport?"

4. **Nǐ cóng nar lái?**
   You from where come = "Where are you from?"

5. **Nǐ péngyǒu zài nǎli?**
   Your friends at where = "Where are your friends?"

6. **Nǐ wèishénme bù shuōhuà?**
   You why not speaking = "Why aren't you speaking?"

7. **Xiànzài jǐ diǎnzhōng le?**
   Now what time already = "What's the time now?"

8. **Nǐ shénme shíhou láide?**
   You what hour come = "When did you arrive?"

13 Yes and no

There are no specific words in Chinese for expressing "yes" and "no" in a question. The closest equivalent is **shìde** 是的 "is" and **búshì** 不是 "is not" respectively. Usually, when the Chinese ask a question such as **Nǐ yào qù Běijīng ma?** 你要去北京吗？ "Do you want to go to Beijing?", the person answering uses the same verb. For example, the verb in the question is **qù** 去 "go", thus the answer would be **Wǒ yào qù Běijīng.** 我要去北京。"I want to go to Beijing." To answer in the negative, you add **bù** 不 before the verb used in the sentence, e.g., **Wǒ bùyào qù Běijīng.** 我不要去北京。"I don't want to go to Beijing."

Nǐ lèi bú lèi?
You tired not tired = "Are you tired?"

"Yes" answer: **Hěn lèi.**
Very tired = "Yes, I'm very tired."

"No" answer: **Bú lèi.**
Not tired = "No, I'm not tired."

Nǐ gāoxìng bú gāoxìng?
You happy not happy = "Are you happy?"

"Yes" answer: **Gāoxìng.**
Happy = "Yes, I'm happy."

"No" answer: **Bù gāoxìng.**
Not happy = "No, I'm not happy."

Alternatively you can use the words **duì** 对 meaning "correct" and **bùduì** 不对 "not correct" (often shortened to **bù** 不 "no") in replics. For example:

Nǐ shì Měiguórén ma?
You are American (question marker) = "Are you American?"

Duì, wǒ shì Měiguórén
Correct, I am American = "Yes, I'm American" or

Bù, wǒ shì Yīngguórén
No, I am British = "No, I'm British."

1. The Basics

 ## Personal details

In China the family name comes first and the given name next. Titles come after the name. For example, Mr Wang is **Wáng xiān-sheng** 王先生 and Ms Wang is **Wáng xiǎojie** 王小姐. The title **tàitai** 太太 is given to married women and is placed after the husband's surname. This is the convention still used by Chinese women in Hong Kong, Macau, Taiwan and outside China. In Mainland China, however, Chinese women now do not adopt their husband's surname after marriage. Overseas Chinese and foreigners will have to get used to this new convention and address married women by their maiden name, e.g., if her surname is **Lǐ** 李 she should be addressed as **Lǐ xiǎojie** 李小姐 or **Lǐ nǚshì** 李女士 (for an older woman). However, you may also use the older title **tàitai** 太太 after the husband's surname in formal situations.

surname	**xìng** 姓
first name	**míngzi** 名字
initials	**xìngmíng suōxiě** 姓名缩写
address	**dìzhǐ** 地址
street	**jiē** 街
unit number	**ménpáihào** 门牌号

postal code	**yóubiān** 邮编
town	**chéngshì** 城市
sex (gender)	**xìngbié** 性别
male	**nán** 男
female	**nǚ** 女
nationality/citizenship	**guójí** 国籍
date of birth	**chūshēng rìqī** 出生日期
place of birth	**chūshēng dìdiǎn** 出生地点
occupation	**zhíyè** 职业
marital status	**hūnyīn zhuàngkuàng** 婚姻状况
married	**yǐhūn** 已婚
single	**wèihūn** 未婚
widow	**guǎfù** 寡妇
widower	**guānfū** 鳏夫
(number of) children	**érnǚ (shùmù)** 儿女〔数目〕
passport	**hùzhào** 护照
identity card	**shēnfènzhèng** 身份证
driving license number	**jiàshǐzhízhào hàomǎ** 驾驶执照号码
place and date of issue	**qiānfā dìdiǎn** 签发地点
date of issue	**qiānfā rìqī** 签发日期
signature	**qiānmíng** 签名

1.2 Today or tomorrow?

What day is it today?	**Jīntiān shì xīngqíjǐ?** 今天是星期几?

Today's Monday.	**Jīntiān shì xīngqíyī.** 今天是星期一。
Tuesday	**Xīngqí'èr** 星期二
Wednesday	**Xīngqísān** 星期三
Thursday	**Xīngqísì** 星期四
Friday	**Xīngqíwǔ** 星期五
Saturday	**Xīngqíliù** 星期六
Sunday	**Xīngqítiān/Xīngqírì** 星期天／星期日
in January	**zài Yīyuè** 在 一月
since February	**Èryuè yǐlái** 二月以来
in spring	**zài chūntiān** 在 春天
in summer	**zài xiàtiān** 在 夏天
in autumn	**zài qiūtiān** 在 秋天
in winter	**zài dōngtiān** 在 冬天
2017	**èrlíngyīqī nián** 二零一七年
the twentieth century	**èrshí shìjì** 20 世纪
the twenty-first century	**èrshíyī shìjì** 21 世纪
What's the date today?	**Jīntiān jǐhào?** 今天几号？
Today's the 24th.	**Jīntiān shì èrshísì hào.** 今天是24号。
Wednesday 3 November	**Shíyīyuè sānhào, xīngqísān** 十一月三号，星期三
in the morning	**zài zǎoshang** 在 早上
in the afternoon	**zài xiàwǔ** 在 下午
in the evening	**zài wǎnshang** 在 晚上
at night	**zài yèlǐ** 在 夜里
this morning	**jīntiān zǎoshang** 今天早上

English	Pinyin	Chinese
this afternoon	**jīntiān xiàwǔ**	今天下午
this evening	**jīntiān bàngwǎn**	今天傍晚
tonight	**jīntiān wǎnshang**	今天晚上
last night	**zuótiān wǎnshang**	昨天晚上
tomorrow night	**míngtiān wǎnshang**	明天晚上
this week	**zhè ge xīngqí**	这个星期
last week	**shàng ge xīngqí**	上个星期
next week	**xià ge xīngqí**	下个星期
this month	**zhè ge yuè**	这个月
last month	**shàng ge yuè**	上个月
next month	**xià ge yuè**	下个月
this year	**jīnnián**	今年
last year	**qùnián**	去年
next year	**míngnián**	明年
in...days	**...tiān yǐhòu**	…天 以后
in...weeks	**...xīngqí yǐhòu**	…星期 以后
in..months	**...yuè yǐhòu**	…月 以后
in...years	**...nián yǐhòu**	…年 以后
...weeks ago	**...(ge) xīngqí yǐqián**	…（个）星期 以前
two weeks ago	**liǎng ge xīngqí yǐqián**	两个星期以前
day off	**xiūjiàrì**	休假日

1.3 What time is it?

What time is it?	**Jǐdiǎn (zhōng) le?/Shénme shíhoule?** 几点(钟)了/什么时候了?
It's nine o'clock.	**Jiǔ diǎn.** 九点
five past ten	**shí diǎn wǔfēn** 十点五分
a quarter past eleven	**shíyī diǎn yī kè** 十一点一刻
fifteen minutes past eleven	**shíyī diǎn shíwǔ fēn** 十一点十五分
twenty past twelve	**shí'èr diǎn èrshí fēn** 十二点二十分
half past one	**yí diǎn bàn** 一点半
twenty-five to three	**liǎng diǎn sānshíwǔ fēn** 两点三十五分
a quarter to four	**sān diǎn sān kè** 三点三刻
ten to five	**sì diǎn wǔshí fēn** 四点五十分
It's noon.	**Zhōngwǔ le.** 中午了。
It's 12 p.m.	**Shí'èr diǎn le.** 十二点了。
It's midnight.	**wǔyè shí'èr diǎn.** 午夜十二点。
half an hour	**bàn ge zhōngtóu** 半个钟头
What time?	**Jǐ diǎn/Shénme shíhou?** 几点/什么时候?
What time can I come by?	**Wǒ jǐ diǎn kěyǐ guòlái?** 我几点可以过来?
at...	**zài...** 在…
after...	**...yǐhòu** …以后
before...	**...yǐqián** …以前
between 4 and 5 p.m.	**sì diǎn hé wǔ diǎn zhījiān** 四点和五点之间

from...to...	**cóng...dào...** 从…到…
in...minutes	**...fénzhōng yǐhòu** …分钟以后
in an hour	**yí ge xiǎoshí yǐhòu** 一个小时以后
in two hours	**liǎng ge zhōngtóu** 两个钟头以后
in a quarter of an hour	**yí kèzhōng yǐhòu** 一刻钟以后
in three quarters of an hour	**sān kèzhōng yǐhòu** 三刻钟以后
too early	**tài zǎo le** 太早了
too late	**tài wǎn le** 太晚了
on time	**zhǔnshí/ànshí** 准时／按时
summertime (daylight saving)	**xiàlìngshí** 夏令时
wintertime	**dōnglìngshí** 冬令时

1.4 One, two, three...

0 **líng** 零	9 **jiǔ** 九
1 **yī** 一	10 **shí** 十
2 **èr** 二	11 **shíyī** 十一
3 **sān** 三	12 **shí'èr** 十二
4 **sì** 四	13 **shísān** 十三
5 **wǔ** 五	14 **shísì** 十四
6 **liù** 六	15 **shíwǔ** 十五
7 **qī** 七	16 **shíliù** 十六
8 **bā** 八	17 **shíqī** 十七

18	**shíbā**	十八	40	**sìshí** 四十
19	**shíjiǔ**	十九	50	**wǔshí** 五十
20	**èrshí**	二十	60	**liùshí** 六十
21	**èrshíyī**	二十一	70	**qīshí** 七十
22	**èrshí'èr**	二十二	80	**bāshí** 八十
30	**sānshí**	三十	90	**jiǔshí** 九十
31	**sānshíyī**	三十一	100	**yībǎi** 一百

101 **yībǎi líng yī** 一百零一

110 **yībǎi yīshí** 一百一十

111 **yībǎi yīshíyī** 一百一十一

200 **èrbǎi/liǎngbǎi** 二百／两百

300 **sānbǎi** 三百

400 **sìbǎi** 四百

500 **wǔbǎi** 五百

600 **liùbǎi** 六百

700 **qībǎi** 七百

800 **bābǎi** 八百

900 **jiǔbǎi** 九百

1,000 **yīqiān** 一千

1,100 **yīqiān yībǎi** 一千一百

2,000 **èrqiān/liǎngqiān** 二千／两千

10,000 **yīwàn** 一万

100,000 **shíwàn** 十万

1,000,000 **(yī)bǎiwàn** （一）百万

10,000,000 **(yī)qiānwàn** （一）千万

1st **dìyī** 第一

2nd **dì'èr** 第二

3rd **dìsān** 第三

4th **dìsì** 第四

once **yícì** 一次

twice **liǎngcì** 两次

double **liǎngbèi** 两倍

triple **sānbèi** 三倍

half **yíbàn** 一半

a quarter **sìfēnzhīyī** 四分之一

a third **sānfēnzhīyī** 三分之一

some **yìxiē** 一些

a few **jǐge** 几个

2 + 4 = 6 **èr jiā sì děngyú liù** 二加四等于六

4 − 2 = 2 **sì jiǎn èr děngyú èr** 四减二等于二

2 x 4 = 8 **èr chéng sì děngyú bā** 二乘四等于八

4 ÷ 2 = 2 **sì chúyǐ èr děngyú èr** 四除以二等于二

even **shuāngshù** 双数

odd **dānshù** 单数

total **yígòng** 一共

1.5 The weather

Is the weather going to be good? | **Tiānqì huì hǎo ma?** 天气会好吗？

Is the weather going to be bad? | **Tiānqì huì bùhǎo ma?** 天气会不好吗？

Is it going to get colder? | **Tiānqì yào biàn lěng le ba?** 天气要变冷了吧？

Is it going to get hotter? | **Tiānqì yào biàn rè le ba?** 天气要变热了吧？

What temperature is it going to be today? | **Jīntiān qìwēn duōshao dù?** 今天气温多少度？

Is it going to rain today? | **Jīntiān huì xiàyǔ ma?** 今天会下雨吗？

Is there going to be a storm today? | **Jīntiān huì yǒu bàofēngyǔ ma?** 今天会有暴风雨吗？

Is it going to snow today? | **Jīntiān huì xiàxuě ma?** 今天会下雪吗？

Is it going to freeze today? | **Jīntiān huì jiébīng ma?** 今天会结冰吗？

Is the thaw setting in? | **Jiědòng le ma?** 解冻了吗？

Is it going to be foggy today? | **Jīntiān huì qǐwù ma?** 今天会起雾吗？

Is there going to be a thunderstorm? | **Jīntiān huì yǒu léiyǔ ma?** 今天会有雷雨吗？

The weather's changing. | **Tiānqì yào biànle.** 天气要变了。

It's going to be cold. | **Tiānqì yào biàn lěngle.** 天气要变冷了。

What's the weather going to be like today? | **Jīntiān de tiānqì zěnmeyàng?** 今天的天气怎么样？

What's the weather going to be like tomorrow? **Míngtiān de tiānqì zěnmeyàng?** 明天的天气怎么样?

rain **xiàyǔ** 下雨	downpour **bàoyǔ/qīngpén dàyǔ** 暴雨／倾盆大雨	frost **yǒu shuāng** 有霜	sweltering/ muggy **mēn rè** 闷热
heavy rain **dàyǔ** 大雨	cold and damp **yòu lěng yòu cháoshī** 又冷又潮湿	wind **fēng** 风	heatwave **rèlàng** 热浪
sunny **qínglǎng** 晴朗	clear skies **lántiān** 蓝天	storm **bàofēngyǔ** 暴风雨	windy **guāfēngde** 刮风的
very hot **hěn rè** 很热	...degrees (Fahrenheit) **(huáshì) dù** (华氏) 度	humid **cháoshī** 潮湿	sunny day **qíng/ tiānqíng** 晴／天晴
fine **qíngtiān** 晴天	...degrees (Celsius) **(shèshì) dù** (摄氏) 度	cool **liángkuai** 凉快	hurricane **jùfēng** 飓风
ice **bīng** 冰	overnight frost **yèjiān yǒu shuāng** 夜间有霜	stifling **mènrènde** 闷热的	warm **nuǎnhuode** 暖和的
icy **jiébīngde** 结冰的	fog **dàwù** 大雾	snowing **xiàxuě** 下雪	cloudiness **duōyún zhuàngtài** 多云状态
frost **shuāng** 霜	foggy **duōwùde** 多雾的	bleak **yīnlěngde** 阴冷的	overcast **yīntiān** 阴天
frosty **hánlěng** 寒冷	...degrees (below zero) **língxià...dù** 零下…度	cloudy **duōyún** 多云	very strong winds **kuángfēng** 狂风
hail **báozi/bīngbáo** 雹子／冰雹	moderate winds **héfēng** 和风	strong winds **dàfēng** 大风	

1.6 Here, there...

See also 5.1 Asking directions

here	**zhèr** 这儿
over here	**zhèlǐ** 这里
there	**nàr** 那儿
over there	**nàli** 那里
somewhere	**mǒuchù** 某处
everywhere	**dàochù** 到处
far away	**yáoyuǎn** 遥远
nearby	**fùjìn** 附近
(on the) right	**zài yòubiān** 在右边
(on the) left	**zài zuǒbiān** 在左边
to the right of	**kào yòubiān** 靠右边
to the left of	**kào zuǒbiān** 靠左边
straight ahead	**yìzhí wǎng qián** 一直往前
via	**jīngguò/yóu** 经过／由
in	**zài...lǐ** 在…里
to	**dào** 到
on	**zài...shàng** 在…上
under	**zài...xià** 在…下
against	**gēn...xiāngduì** 跟…相对
opposite/facing	**duìmiàn** 对面
next to	**āizhe** 挨着
beside...	**zài...pángbiān** 在…旁边

The Basics

1

near	**kàojìn** 靠近
in front of	**zài...qiánmiàn** 在···前面
in the center	**zài...zhōngjiān** 在···中间
forward	**xiàng qián** 向前
down	**xiàng xià** 向下
up	**xiàng shàng** 向上
inside	**lǐbiān** 里边
outside	**wàibiān** 外边
at the front	**zài...qiánmiàn** 在···前面
at the back	**zài...hòumiàn** 在···后面
in the north	**zài...běibiān** 在···北边
to the south	**zài...yǐ nán** 在···以南
from the west	**(cóng)...xībiān** 〔从〕···西边
from the east	**(cóng)...dōngbiān** 〔从〕···东边

1.7 What does that sign say?

See 5.2 Traffic signs

交通标志 **Jiāotōng Biāozhì** Traffic Signs	邮局 **Yóujú** Post Office	此路不通 **Cǐlù Bùtōng** No Access
出租 **Chūzū** For Hire/Rent	高压电 **Gāo Yā Diàn** High Voltage	禁止入内 **Jìnzhǐ Rùnèi** No Entry
出售 **Chūshòu** For Sale	问讯处 **Wènxùn Chù** Information	警察〔局〕/公安〔局〕 **Jǐngchá (Jú)/Gōng'ān (Jú)** Police Station
卖完 **Màiwán** Sold Out	售票处 **Shòupiào Chù** Ticket Office	交通警察 **Jiāotōng Jǐngchá** Traffic Police

热水
Rèshuǐ
Hot Water

冷水
Lěngshuǐ
Cold Water

非饮用水
Fēiyǐnyòngshuǐ
Water (Not For
  Drinking)

停用
Tíngyòng
Not In Use

推
Tuī
Push

开
Kāi
Open

拉
Lā
Pull

洗手间
Xǐshǒujiān
Bathrooms

满／客满
Mǎn/Kèmǎn
Full

预订席／包席
Yùdìngxí/Bāoxí
Reserved

宾馆／旅馆
Bīn'guǎn/Lǚguǎn
Hotel

待维修
Dài Wéixiū
Out of Order

收款处
Shōukuǎn Chù
Cashier

免费入场
Miǎnfèi Rùchǎng
Free Entrance

当心恶狗
Dāngxīn è Gǒu
Beware of the Dog

油漆未干
Yóuqī Wèi Gān
Wet Paint

无人
Wúrén
Vacant

入口
Rùkǒu
Entrance

紧急出口
Jǐnjí Chūkǒu
(Emergency) Exit

有人
Yǒurén
Engaged

行人
Xíngrén
Pedestrians

时刻表
Shíkèbiǎo
Timetable

兑换
Duìhuàn
Exchange

危险
Wēixiǎn
Danger

医院
Yīyuàn
Hospital

急救室
Jíjiùshì
First Aid (Hospital)

事故急诊室
Shìgù Jízhěnshì
Accident and Emergency
  (Hospital)

消防局
Xiāofángjú
Fire Station

自动扶梯
Zìdòng fútī
Escalator

安全出口
Ānquán Chūkǒu
Fire Escape

旅行咨询处
Lǚxíng Zīxúnchù
Tourist Information Bureau

请勿抽烟
Qǐngwù Chōuyān
No Smoking

请勿乱丢垃圾
Qǐngwù Luàndiū Lājī
No Littering

易燃
Yìrán
Fire Hazard

请勿打扰
Qǐngwù Dǎrǎo
Please Do Not Disturb

请勿触摸
Qǐngwù Chùmō
Please Do Not Touch

停（止） **Tíng (Zhǐ)** Stop	禁止钓鱼 **Jìnzhǐ Diàoyǘ** No Fishing	紧急刹车 **Jǐnjíshāchē** Emergency Brake
候机／候车室 **Hóujī/Hóuchē** Waiting Room	禁止打猎 **Jìnzhǐ Dǎliè** No Hunting	致命 **Zhìmìng** Danger to Life

1.8 Legal holidays

Apart from Chinese New Year which is celebrated throughout China with one week off from work, other holidays are mostly observed in the cities with time off to celebrate the festivities. There are two types of festivals, traditional and modern.

The former follow the lunar calendar which identifies the months sequentially as the First Month, the Second Month, etc. Chinese New Year or the Spring Festival varies every year but falls between the last ten days of January and the first ten days of February each year.

Modern holidays in China include National Day (October 1) and Labor Day (May 1). National Day and Labor Day are cele-brated with a week and three days off work respectively, when people are encouraged to spend and go for holidays in an attempt to stimulate the economy. On these occasions, govern-ment institutions and head offices of banks are closed for busi-ness. However, local bank branches are open for about five hours a day for one to three days. Shopping centers are open till mid-night while supermarkets and medium-sized shops keep normal opening hours. Local shops and convenience stores vary, some might operate for fewer hours during the holidays.

January 1 **[Yīyuè yīhào]**: New Year's Day **Xīnnián/Yuándàn**
新年/元旦

January/February (Lunar Calendar: First Day of the First Month)
[Nónglì Zhēngyuè Chūyī]: Chinese New Year **Chūnjié** 春节

January/February (Lunar Calendar: Fifteenth Day of the First Month) **[Nónglì Zhēngyuè shíwǔrì]**: The Lantern Festival **Yuánxiāojié** 元宵节

March 8 **[Sānyuè bāhào]**: Women's Day **Fùnǚjié** 妇女节

April 2-4 (Usually the 15th day after the Spring Equinox, date may vary) **[Sìyuè èr-sìhào]**: Festival of Sweeping Ancestors' Graves **Qīngmíngjié** 清明节

May 1 **[Wǔyuè yīhào]**: Labor Day **Láodòngjié** 劳动节

May 4 **[Wǔyuè sìhào]**: Youth Festival **Qīngniánjié** 青年节

June 1 **[Liùyuè yīhào]**: Children's Day **Értóngjié** 儿童节

June (Lunar Calendar: Fifth Day of the Fifth Month) **[Nónglì Wǔyuè wǔrì]**: Dragon Boat Festival **Duānwǔjié** 端午节

July 1 **[Qīyuè yīhào]**: Foundation Day of Chinese Communist Party **Jiàndǎngjié** 建党节

August 1 **[Bāyuè yīhào]**: Foundation Day of the People's Liberation Army **Jiànjūnjié** 建军节

September/October (Lunar Calendar: Fifth Day of the Eighth Month) **[Nónglì Bāyuè shíwǔrì]**: The Mid-Autumn Festival **Zhōngqiūjié** 中秋节

October 1 **[Shíyuè yīhào]**: National Day **Guóqìngjié** 国庆节

2. Meet and Greet

It is normal in China to shake hands on meeting and parting company. The strength of the handshake is determined by the level of acquaintance and the importance of the occasion. Generally one should refrain from giving a strong handshake unless you know the person well already. Hugging is reserved for relatives and kissing on the cheeks is rarely seen among Chinese except on occasions involving foreigners.

2.1 Greetings

Hello Mr Williams.	**Nǐ hǎo, Wēiliánmǔsī xiānsheng.** 你好，威廉姆斯先生。
Good morning, Mr Williams.	**Zǎo, Wēiliánmǔsī xiānsheng.** 早，威廉姆斯先生。
Hello Mrs Jones.	**Nǐ hǎo, Qióngsī tàitai.** 你好，琼斯太太。
Good morning, Mrs Jones.	**Zǎo, Qióngsī fūren.** 早，琼斯夫人。
Hello, Peter.	**Nǐ hǎo, Bǐdé.** 你好，彼德。
Hi, Helen.	**Nǐ hǎo, Kǎilún.** 你好，凯伦。
Good morning, madam.	**Zǎoshang hǎo, tàitai/fūren.** 早上好，太太／夫人。
Good afternoon, sir.	**Xiàwǔ hǎo, xiānsheng.** 下午好，先生。

Good evening.	**Wǎnshang hǎo.** 晚上好。
How are you?	**Nǐ hǎo ma?** 你好吗？
How's everything?	**Zěnmeyàng?** 怎么样？
Fine, thank you, and you?	**Hái hǎo, xièxie, nǐ ne?** 还好，谢谢，你呢？
Very well, and you?	**Hěn hǎo, nǐ ne?** 很好，你呢？
In excellent health	**Jīngshén hǎo** 精神好
In great shape	**Shēntǐ hǎo** 身体好
So-so	**Mǎmǎhūhū** 马马虎虎
Not very well	**Bù zěnme hǎo** 不怎么好
Not bad	**Búcuò** 不错
I'm going to leave.	**Wǒ yào zǒu le.** 我要走了。
I have to be going, someone's waiting for me.	**Wǒ děi zǒu le, yǒu rén zài děng wǒ.** 我得走了，有人在等我。
Good-bye.	**Zàijiàn.** 再见。
See you later.	**Yìhuǐr jiàn.** 一会儿见。
See you in a little while.	**Dāi huǐr jiàn.** 待会儿见。
Sweet dreams.	**Zuò ge hǎo mèng.** 做个好梦。
Good night.	**Wǎn'ān.** 晚安。
All the best/Good luck.	**Zhù nǐ hǎo yùn.** 祝你好运。
Have fun.	**Wánr kāixīn diǎnr.** 玩开心点儿。
Have a nice vacation.	**Jiàqī yúkuài.** 假期愉快。
Have a good weekend.	**Zhōumò yúkuài.** 周末愉快。
Bon voyage.	**Yī lù píng'ān.** 一路平安。
Have a good trip.	**Lǚtú yúkuài.** 旅途愉快。

Thank you, the same to you.	**Xièxie, nǐ yě yíyàng.** 谢谢，你也一样。
Say hello to...	**Dài...wèn hǎo** 代…问好
Give my regards to... [formal]	**Qǐng nǐ dài wǒ xiàng...wèn hǎo** 请你代我向…问好
Say hello to… [informal]	**Xiàng...wèn hǎo** 向…问好

2.2 Asking a question

Who?	**Shéi?** 谁？
Who's that?	**Shì shéi?** 是谁？
Who are you?	**Nín shì shéi?** 您是谁？
What?	**Shénme?** 什么？
What is there to see?	**Yǒu shénme hǎo kàn de?** 有什么好看的？
Where?	**Nǎr/Nǎli?** 哪儿？／哪里？
Where's the bathroom?	**Cèsuǒ zài nǎr/nǎli?** 厕所在哪儿／哪里？
Where are you going?	**Nǐ shàng nǎr/nǎli qù?** 你上哪儿／哪里去？
Where are you from?	**Nǐ cóng nǎr/nǎli lái?** 你从哪儿／哪里来？
What?	**Shénme?** 什么？
How?	**Zěnme?** 怎么？
What's your surname? [formal]	**Nǐ guì xìng?** 您贵姓？
What's your name?	[formal] **Zěnme chēnghū nín?** 怎么称呼您？
	[informal] **Nǐ jiào shénme míngzi?** 你叫什么名字？

How far is that?	**Yào duō yuǎn?** 要多远?
How long does that take?	**Yào duō jiǔ?** 要多久?
How long is the trip?	**Lùchéng yào duō jiǔ?** 路程要多久?
How much?	**Duōshao qián?** 多少钱?
How much is this?	**Zhè ge duōshao qián?** 这个多少钱?
What time is it?	**Jǐ diǎn le?** 几点了?
Which one?	**Nǎ ge** 哪个?
Which ones?	**Nǎ xiē?** 哪些?
Which glass is mine?	**Nǎ ge bēizi shì wǒde?** 哪个杯子是我的?
When?	**Shénme shíhou?** 什么时候?
When are you leaving? [formal]	**Nǐ shénme shíhou chūfā?** 你什么时候出发?
Why?	**Wèishénme?** 为什么?
Could you...? [formal]	**Kě bu kěyǐ...?** 可不可以…?
Please... [formal]	**Qǐng...** 请…
Are you able to...? [informal]	**Néng...ma?** 能…吗?
Could you...? [informal]	**Kěyǐ...ma?** 可以…吗?
Could you help me, please?	**Nǐ kěyǐ bāngzhu wǒ ma?** 你可以帮助我吗?
Could you show that to me, please?	**Qǐng zhǐ gěi wǒ kàn.** 请指给我看。
Could you come with me, please?	**Qǐng gén wǒ lái.** 请跟我来。
Could you book some tickets for me please?	**Qǐng gěi wǒ yùdìng jǐ zhāng piào.** 请给我预订几张票。

Could you recommend another hotel?	**Qǐng gěi wǒ tuījiàn lìngwài yī jiā lǚguǎn, hǎo ma?** 请给我推荐另外一家旅馆，好吗？
What category of hotel is it? (How many stars)	**Zhè jiā lǚguǎn shì jǐ xīng jí de?** 这家旅馆是几星级的？
Do you know...? [formal]	**Nǐ zhī bu zhīdao...?** 你知不知道…？
Do you have...?	**Yǒu méiyǒu...?** 有没有…？
Do you have any vegetarian dishes, please?	**Qǐngwèn, yǒu méiyǒu sùshí de cài?** 请问，有没有素食的菜？
I would like a...	**Wǒ yào yí ge...** 我要一个…
I'd like a kilo of apples, please.	**Qǐng gěi wǒ yī gōngjīn píngguǒ.** 请给我一公斤苹果。
Can I?	**Wǒ kěyǐ...?** 我可以…？
May I take this away?	**Wǒ kěyǐ názǒu zhège ma?** 我可以拿走这个吗？
Can I smoke here?	**Wǒ kěyǐ zài zhèlǐ chōuyān ma?** 我可以在这里抽烟吗？
Could I ask you something?	**Kěyǐ wèn nín jiàn shìr ma?** 可以问您件事儿吗？

2.3 How to Reply

My surname is ...	**Wǒ xìng...** 我姓…
My name is ...	**Wǒ jiào...** 我叫…
Yes, of course.	**Shì, dāngrán.** 是，当然。
No, I'm sorry.	**Bú, duìbuqǐ.** 不，对不起。
Yes, what can I do for you?	**Duì, zháo wǒ yǒu shìr ma?** 对，找我有事儿吗？
Just a moment, please.	**Qǐng děng yìhuǐr.** 请等一会儿。

No, I don't have time now.	**Duìbuqǐ, wǒ xiànzài méiyǒu kòngr.** 对不起，我现在没有空儿。
No, that's impossible.	**Duìbuqǐ, bànbudào.** 对不起，办不到。
No problem.	**Méi wèntí.** 没问题。
I agree.	**Wǒ tóngyì.** 我同意。
I hope so too.	**Wǒ yě dànyuàn shì zhèyàng.** 我也但愿是这样。
No, not at all.	**Bù, búshì zhèyàng.** 不，不是这样。
No, nothing.	**Bù, méiyǒu.** 不，没有。
That's right!	**Duì!** 对！
Something's wrong.	**Chūshì le.** 出事了。
There's a problem.	**Chū wèntí le.** 出问题了。
I agree.	**Wǒ tóngyì.** 我同意。
I don't agree.	**Wǒ bù tóngyì.** 我不同意。
OK/It's fine.	**Hǎo, méiyǒu wèntí.** 好，没有问题。
OK, all right.	**Hǎo, jiù zhèyàng.** 好，就这样。
Perhaps/maybe	**Yěxǔ** 也许
Maybe	**Kěněng** 可能
I don't know.	**Wǒ bù zhīdao.** 我不知道。

2.4 Thank you

Thank you.	**Xièxie.** 谢谢。
Don't mention it.	**Bú kèqi.** 不客气。
Thank you very much.	**Fēicháng gǎnxiè.** 非常感谢。
Very kind of you.	**Nín tài kèqi le.** 您太客气了。

My pleasure.	**Wǒde róngxìng.** 我的荣幸。
I enjoyed it very much.	**Wǒ fēicháng xǐhuan.** 我非常喜欢。
Thank you for...	**Xièxie nǐ gěi wǒ...** 谢谢你给我···
That was so kind of you.	**Nǐ tài kèqi le.** 你太客气了。
Don't mention it.	**Búyòng xiè.** 不用谢。

 I'm sorry

Excuse me (asking a question)	**Qǐng wèn** 请问
Sorry	**Duìbuqǐ** 对不起
Excuse me [polite]	**Qǐng wèn yíxià** 请问一下
Sorry to bother you.	**Máfan nǐ le.** 麻烦你了。
Sorry to bother you. [polite]	**Bùhǎoyìsī, dǎráo nǐ le.** 不好意思，打扰你了。
Sorry, I didn't know that...	**Duìbuqǐ, wǒ bù zhīdao ...** 对不起，我不知道···
I do apologize.	[formal] **Wǒ zhēnchéng dàoqiàn.** 我真诚道歉。
	[informal] **Tài duìbuqǐ le.** 太对不起了。
I didn't mean it.	**Wǒ búshì gùyì de.** 我不是故意的。
It was an accident.	**Zhè shì ge yìwài.** 这是个意外。
That's all right. [formal]	**Bú yàojǐn.** 不要紧。
Don't worry about it. [formal]	**Méi guānxi.** 没关系。
Never mind. [informal]	**Bú ài'shì.** 不碍事。
It's okay. [informal]	**Méi shì.** 没事。

It could happen to anyone.

Shéi yě miǎnbuliǎo. 谁也免不了。

2.6 What do you think?

Which do you prefer? [formal]

Nǐ xǐhuan nǎ ge? 你喜欢哪个？

Which do you like best? [formal]

Nǐ zuì xǐhuan nǎ ge? 你最喜欢哪个？

What do you think? [informal]

Nǐ juéde zěnmeyàng? 你觉得怎么样？

Don't you like dancing?

Nǐ bù xǐhuan tiàowǔ ma?
你不喜欢跳舞吗？

I don't mind.

Wǒ wúsuǒwèi. 我无所谓。

Well done!

Tài bàng le! 太棒了！

Not bad!

Búcuò! 不错！

Great!/Marvelous!

Hǎojíle! 好极了！

Wonderful!

Tài hǎo le! 太好了！

I am pleased for you.

[formal] **Wǒ wèi nǐ gāoxìng.**
我为你高兴。

[informal] **Wǒ tì nǐ gāoxìng.**
我替你高兴。

I'm very happy to...

....wǒ hěn gāoxìng ⋯我很高兴

It's really nice here!

Zhèlǐ jiǎnzhí tài hǎo le!
这里简直太好了！

How nice!

Zhēn hǎo! 真好！

I'm very happy with...

Wǒ duì...hěn mǎnyǐ 我对⋯很满意

I'm not very happy with...

Wǒ duì...bù mǎnyì 我对⋯不满意

I'm glad that....

Wǒ wèi...gāoxìng 我为⋯高兴

Meet and Greet

2

I'm having a great time.	**Wǒ wánrde hěn gāoxìng.** 我玩儿得很高兴。
I can't wait till tomorrow.	**Wǒ kě děngbudào míngtiān la.** 我可等不到明天啦。
I'm looking forward to tomorrow.	**Wǒ qīdàizhe míngtiān de láilín.** 我期待着明天的来临。
I hope it works out.	**Wǒ xīwàng yíqiè jìnxíng shùnlì.** 我希望一切进行顺利。
How awful!	**Tài zāogāo le!** 太糟糕了!
It's horrible!	**Tài kǒngbù le!** 太恐怖了!
That's terrible!	**Tài kěpà le!** 太可怕了!
What a pity/shame!	**Zhēn kěxī!** 真可惜!
How disgusting!	**Zhēn ěxīn!** 真恶心!
What nonsense!	**Shuō shénme fèihuà!** 说什么废话!
How silly!	**Zhēn shì húnào!** 真是胡闹!
That's ridiculous!	**Tài kěxiào le!** 太可笑了!
I don't like it.	**Wǒ bù xǐhuan.** 我不喜欢。
I'm bored to death!	**Mènsǐ le!** 闷死了!
I'm fed up!	**Fánsǐ rén le!** 烦死人了!
This is no good.	**Zhè kě bù hǎo.** 这可不好。
This is not what I expected.	**Wǒ kě méi xiǎngdào huì zhèyàng.** 我可没想到会这样。

3. Small Talk

3.1 Introductions

My name's...	**Wǒ jiào...** 我叫⋯
I'm...	**Wǒ shì...** 我是⋯
What's your name?	[formal] **Qǐngwèn, nín guìxìng?** 请问, 您贵姓?
	[informal] **Nǐ jiào shénme míngzi?** 你叫什么名字?
May I introduce...?	**Wǒ lái jièshào, zhè shì..., zhè shì...** 我来介绍, 这是⋯, 这是⋯
This is my wife.	**Zhè shì wǒ qīzi.** 这是我妻子。
This is my husband.	**Zhè shì wǒ zhàngfu.** 这是我丈夫。
This is my daughter.	**Zhè shì wǒ nǚ'ér.** 这是我女儿。
This is my son.	**Zhè shì wǒ érzi.** 这是我儿子。
This is my mother.	[formal] **Zhè shì wǒ mǔqin.** 这是我母亲。
	[informal] **Zhè shì wǒ mā.** 这是我妈。

This is my father.	[formal] **Zhè shì wǒ fùqin.** 这是我父亲。
	[informal] **Zhè shì wǒ bà.** 这是我爸。
This is my fiancée.	**Zhè shì wǒ wèihūnqī.** 这是我未婚妻。
This is my fiancé.	**Zhè shì wǒ wèihūnfū.** 这是我未婚夫。
This is my girlfriend.	**Zhè shì wǒ nǚpéngyou.** 这是我女朋友。
This is my boyfriend.	**Zhè shì wǒ nánpéngyou.** 这是我女朋友。
This is my friend.	**Zhè shì wǒ péngyou.** 这是我朋友。
How do you do?	**Nǐ hǎo!** 你好!
Pleased to meet you. [formal]	**Rènshi nǐ hěn gāoxìng.** 认识你很高兴。
Hi, pleased to meet you.	**Nǐ hǎo, rènshi nǐ hěn gāoxìng.** 你好, 认识你很高兴。
It's a pleasure (honor).	**Xìnghuì, xìnghuì!** 幸会, 幸会!
Where are you from?	[formal] **Nǐ shì nǎguórén?** 你是哪国人?
	[informal] **Nǐ cóng nǎli lái?** 你从哪里来?
I'm American.	**Wǒ cóng Měiguó lái.** 我从美国来。
I'm British.	**Wǒ cóng Yīngguó lái.** 我从英国来。
I'm Canadian.	**Wǒ cóng Jiānádà lái.** 我从加拿大来。
I'm Singaporean.	**Wǒ cóng Xīngjiāpō lái.** 我从新加坡来。
I'm Australian.	**Wǒ cóng Àodàlìyà lái.** 我从澳大利亚来。
What city do you live in?	**Nǐ zhù zài nǎ ge chéngshì?** 你住在哪个城市?
In..	**Zài...** 在…

Near...	Kàojìn... 靠近…
How long have you been here?	Nǐ lái zhèlǐ duō jiǔ le? 你来这里多久了?
A few days.	Zhǐ yǒu jǐ tiān. 只有几天。
How long will you be staying here?	Nǐ yào zài zhèr zhù duō jiǔ? 你要在这儿住多久?
We'll (probably) be leaving tomorrow.	Wǒmen (kěnéng) míngtiān zǒu. 我们(可能)明天走。
We'll (probably) be leaving in two weeks.	Wǒmen (kěnéng) guò liǎng ge xīngqí zǒu. 我们(可能)过两个星期走。
Where are you staying?	Nǐ zhù zài nǎr? 你住在哪儿?
I'm staying in a hotel.	Wǒ zhù zài yī jiā lǚguǎn. 我住在一家旅馆。
I'm staying with friends.	Wǒ zhù zài péngyou jiā. 我住在朋友家。
I'm staying with relatives.	Wǒ zhù zài qīnqi jiā. 我住在亲戚家。
Are you here by yourself?	Nǐ yí ge rén lái ma? 你一个人来吗?
Are you here with your family?	Nǐ gēn jiārén lái ma? 你跟家人来吗?
I'm on my own.	Wǒ yí ge rén lái. 我一个人来。
I came with my wife.	Wǒ gēn wǒ qīzi lái. 我跟我妻子来。
I came with my husband.	Wǒ gēn wǒ zhàngfu lái. 我跟我丈夫来。
I came with my family.	Wǒ gēn jiārén lái. 我跟家人来。
I came with my relatives.	Wǒ gēn qīngqi lái. 我跟亲戚来。
I came with a friend(s).	Wǒ gēn péngyou lái. 我跟朋友来。
Are you married?	Nǐ jiéhūn le méiyǒu? 你结婚了没有?

Do you have a steady boyfriend?	**Nǐ yǒu nánpéngyou méiyǒu?** 你有男朋友没有？
Do you have a steady girlfriend?	**Nǐ yǒu nǚpéngyou méiyǒu?** 你有女朋友没有？
I'm married.	**Wǒ jiéhūn le.** 我结婚了。
I'm single.	**Wǒ dānshēn.** 我单身。
I'm not married.	**Wǒ méi jiéhūn.** 我没结婚。
I'm separated (from my wife).	**Wǒ gēn wǒ qīzi fēnjū le.** 我跟我妻子分居了。
I'm separated (from (my husband).	**Wǒ gēn wǒ zhàngfu fēnjū le.** 我跟我丈夫分居了。
I'm divorced.	**Wǒ líhūn le.** 我离婚了。
I'm a widow.	**Wǒ de zhàngfu qùshì le.** 我的丈夫去世了。
I'm a widower.	**Wǒ de qīzi qùshì le.** 我的妻子去世了。
I live alone.	**Wǒ yí ge rén zhù.** 我一个人住。
Do you have any children?	**Nǐ yǒu méiyǒu háizi?** 你有没有孩子？
Do you have any grandchildren?	**Nǐ yǒu méiyǒu sūnzi?** 你有没有孙子？
How old are you?	[addressing young people] **Nǐ duō dà le?** 你多大了？
	[addressing older people, informal] **Nín jīnnián duō dà le?** 您今年多大了？
	[addressing older people, formal] **Nín duō dà suìshù/niānjì le?** 您多大岁数／年纪了？
How old is she/he?	**Tā duō dà le?** 她／他多大了？
I'm...(years old)	**Wǒ jīnnián...suì** 我今年…岁
She's/He's...(years old)	**Tā jīnnián...suì** 她／他今年…岁

What do you do for a living?	[formal] **Nǐ zuò shénme gōngzuò?** 你做什么工作？
	[informal] **Nǐ shì zuò shénme de?** 你是做什么的？
I work in an office.	**Wǒ zài bàn gōngshì gōngzuò.** 我在办公室工作。
I'm a student.	**Wǒ shì xuésheng.** 我是学生。
I'm unemployed.	**Wǒ shīyè le.** 我失业了。
I'm retired.	**Wǒ tuìxiū le.** 我退休了。
I'm on a disability pension.	**Wǒ zài lǐng shāngcán fǔxùjīn.** 我在领伤残抚恤金。
I'm a housewife.	**Wǒ shì jiātíng fùnǚ.** 我是家庭妇女。
Do you like your job?	**Nǐ xǐhuan nǐde gōngzuò ma?** 你喜欢你的工作吗？
Most of the time.	**Dà duō shíhou xǐhuan.** 大多时候喜欢。
Mostly I do, but I prefer vacations.	**Wǒ xǐhuan wǒde gōngzuò, búguò wǒ gèng xǐhuan fàngjià.** 我喜欢我的工作，不过我更喜欢放假。

3.2 I beg your pardon?

I don't speak any...	**Wǒ bú huì shuō...** 我不会说…
I speak a little...	**Wǒ huì shuō yìdiǎn...** 我会说一点…
I'm American.	**Wǒ shì Měiguórén.** 我是美国人。
I'm British.	**Wǒ shì Yīngguórén.** 我是英国人。
I'm Canadian.	**Wǒ shì Jiānádàrén.** 我是加拿大人。
I'm Singaporean.	**Wǒ shì Xīngjiāpōrén.** 我是新加坡人。
I'm Australian.	**Wǒ shì Àodàlìyàrén.** 我是澳大利亚人。

Do you speak English?	**Nǐ huì shuō Yīngyǔ ma?** 你会说英语吗?
Is there anyone who speaks...?	**Zhèlǐ yǒu méiyǒu rén huì shuō...?** 这里有没有人会说…?
What?	**Shénme?** 什么?
I (don't) understand.	**Wǒ (bù) dǒng.** 我(不)懂。
Do you understand me?	**Nǐ dǒng wǒ shuō de huà ma?** 你懂我说的话吗?
Could you repeat that, please?	**Qǐng nǐ zài shuō yí biàn.** 请你再说一遍。
Could you speak more slowly, please?	**Qǐng nǐ shuō màn yìdiǎn.** 请你说慢一点。
What does this mean?	**Zhè shì shénme yìsi?** 这是什么意思?
What does that mean?	**Nà shì shénme yìsi?** 那是什么意思?
It's more or less the same as...	**Zhè gēn...chàbuduō yíyàng** 这跟…差不多一样
Could you write that down for me, please?	**Qǐng gěi wǒ xiěxiàlai.** 请给我写下来。
Could you spell that for me, please?	**Qǐng yòng zìmǔ pīnchūlai.** 请用字母拼出来。
Could you point to the phrase in this book, please?	**Qǐng zài zhè běn shū lǐ zhǐchū zhè jù huà.** 请在这本书里指出这句话。
Just a minute, I'll look it up.	**Qǐng děngyiděng, wǒ chácha.** 请等一等,我查查。
I can't find the word.	**Wǒ zhǎobudào zhè ge cí.** 我找不到这个词。
I can't find the sentence.	**Wǒ zhǎobudào zhè ge jùzi.** 我找不到这个句子。

| How do you say that in...? | **...zěnme shuō?** ⋯怎么说? |
| How do you pronounce that word? | **Zhè ge cí zěnme niàn?** 这个词怎么念? |

3.3 Starting/ending a conversation

Could I ask you something?	**Wǒ kěyǐ wèn nǐ yí jiàn shì ma?** 我可以问你一件事吗?
Could you help me please?	**Kěyǐ bāng ge máng ma?** 可以帮个忙吗?
Yes, what's the problem?	**Kěyǐ, yǒu shénme shì?** 可以，有什么事?
What can I do for you?	**Yǒu shénme wǒ kěyǐ bāng nǐ de?** 有什么我可以帮你的?
Sorry, I don't have time now.	**Duìbuqǐ wǒ xiànzài méi kòngr.** 对不起，我现在没空儿。
Do you have a light?	**Yǒu méiyǒu dǎhuǒjī?** 有没有打火机?
May I join you?	**Wǒ kěyǐ jirù (nǐmen) ma?** 我可以加入〔你们〕吗?
Can I take a picture?	**Wǒ kěyǐ zhào zhāng xiàng ma?** 我可以照张相吗?
Could you take a picture of me?	**Nǐ kěyǐ gěi wǒ zhào zhāng xiàng ma?** 你可以给我照张相吗?
Could you take a picture of us?	**Nǐ kěyǐ gěi wǒmen zhào zhāng xiàng ma?** 你可以给我们照张相吗?
Leave me alone.	**Bié chánzhe wǒ.** 别缠着我。
Leave me alone. (polite)	**Ràng wǒ jìng yíxià.** 让我静一下。
Go away!	**Zǒukāi!** 走开!
Go away or I'll scream.	**Nǐ zài bù zǒukāi wǒ jiù dàshēng hǎn le.** 你再不走开我就大声喊了。

3.4 A chat about the weather

See also 1.5 The weather

It's so hot today!	**Jīntiān zhēn rè!** 今天真热!
It's so cold today!	**Jīntiān zhēn lěng!** 今天真冷!
Isn't it a lovely day?	**Jīntiān tiānqì tài hǎo le!** 今天天气太好了!
It's so windy!	**Fēng tài dà le!** 风太大了!
What a storm!	**Guā dàfēng le!** 刮大风了!
All that rain!	**Xià zhème dà de yǔ!** 下这么大的雨!
All that snow!	**Xià zhème dà de xuě!** 下这么大的雪!
It's so foggy!	**Qǐ zhème dà de wù!** 起这么大的雾!
Has the weather been like this for long?	**Zhèyàng de tiānqì hěn jiǔ le ma?** 这样的天气很久了吗?
Is it always this hot here?	**Zhèlǐ zǒngshì zhème rè ma?** 这里总是这么热吗?
Is it always this cold here?	**Zhèlǐ zǒngshì zhème lěng ma?** 这里总是这么冷吗?
Is it always this dry here?	**Zhèlǐ zǒngshì zhème gānzào ma?** 这里总是这么干燥吗?
Is it always this humid here?	**Zhèlǐ zǒngshì zhème cháoshī ma?** 这里总是这么潮湿吗?

3.5 Hobbies

Do you have any hobbies?	**Nǐ yǒu shénme àihào?** 你有什么爱好?
I like reading.	**Wǒ xǐhuan kànshū.** 我喜欢看书。
I like photography.	**Wǒ xǐhuan shèyǐng.** 我喜欢摄影。

I enjoy listening to music.	**Wǒ xǐhuan tīng yīnyuè.** 我喜欢听音乐。
I play the guitar.	**Wǒ xǐhuan tán jítā.** 我喜欢弹吉他。
I play the piano.	**Wǒ xǐhuan tán gāngqín.** 我喜欢弹钢琴。
I like watching movies.	**Wǒ xǐhuan kàn diànyǐng.** 我喜欢看电影。
I like traveling.	**Wǒ xǐhuan qù lǚyóu.** 我喜欢去旅游。
I like exercising.	**Wǒ xǐhuan qù yùndòng.** 我喜欢去运动。
I like going fishing.	**Wǒ xǐhuan qù diàoyú.** 我喜欢去钓鱼。
I like going for a walk.	**Wǒ xǐhuan qù sànbù.** 我喜欢去散步。

 **3.6 Invitations**

Are you doing anything tonight?	[formal] **Wǎnshang nǐ yǒu shénme huódòng?** 晚上你有什么活动？
	[informal] **Wǎnshang nǐ xiǎng zuò shénme?** 晚上你想做什么？
Do you have any plans for today?	[formal] **Jīntiān yǒu shénme huódòng?** 今天有什么活动？
	[informal] **Jīntiān nǐ yǒu shénme ānpái?** 今天你有什么安排？
Do you have any plans for this afternoon?	[formal] **Xiàwǔ yǒu shénme huódòng?** 下午有什么活动？
Do you have any plans for tonight?	[informal] **Wǎnshang nǐ yǒu shénme ānpái?** 今天晚上你有什么安排？
Would you like to go out with me?	[formal] **Nǐ xiǎng gēn wǒ wàichū ma?** 你想跟我外出吗？
	[informal] **Gēn wǒ chūqu wánr, zěnmeyàng?** 跟我出去玩儿，怎么样？

Would you like to go dancing with me?	[formal] **Nǐ xiǎng gēn wǒ qù tiàowǔ ma?** 你想跟我去跳舞吗？
	[informal] **Gēn wǒ qù tiàowǔ, zěnmeyàng?** 跟我去跳舞，怎么样？
Would you like to have lunch with me? [formal]	**Nǐ xiǎng gēn wǒ qù chī wǔfàn ma?** 你想跟我去吃午饭吗？
Would you like to have dinner with me? [informal]	**Gēn wǒ qù chī wǎnfàn, zěnmeyàng?** 跟我去吃晚饭，怎么样？
Would you like to come to the beach with me?	[formal] **Nǐ xiǎng gēn wǒ qù hǎitān ma?** 你想跟我去海滩吗？
	[informal] **Gēn wǒ qù hǎitān, zěnmeyàng?** 跟我去海滩，怎么样？
Would you like to come into town with us?	[formal] **Nǐ xiǎng gēn wǒmen jìnchéng ma?** 你想跟我们进城吗？
	[informal] **Gēn wǒmen jìnchéng, zěnmeyàng?** 跟我们进城，怎么样？
Would you like to come and see some friends with us?	[formal] **Nǐ xiǎng gēn wǒmen qù kàn péngyou ma?** 你想跟我们去看朋友吗？
	[informal] **Gēn wǒmen qù kàn péngyou, zěnmeyàng?** 跟我们去看朋友，怎么样？
Shall we dance?	**Tiàowǔ ma?** 跳舞吗？
Shall we sit at the bar?	**Qù jiǔbā zuòzuo?** 去酒吧坐坐？
Shall we get something to drink?	**Hē diǎn shénme yǐnliào?** 喝点什么饮料？
Shall we go for a walk?	**Chūqu zǒuzou?** 出去走走？
Shall we go for a drive?	**Kāichē guàngyiguàng?** 开车逛一逛？
Yes, all right.	**Hǎo a.** 好啊。
Good idea.	**Hǎo zhǔyì.** 好主意。

No, thank you.	**Bùle, xièxie.** 不了, 谢谢。
Maybe later.	**Wǎn diǎnr ba.** 晚点儿吧。
I don't feel like it.	**Wǒ méiyǒu xìngqù.** 我没有兴趣。
I don't have time.	**Wǒ méiyǒu kòngr.** 我没有空儿。
I already have a date.	**Wǒ yǐjīng yǒu yuēhuì le.** 我已经有约会了。
I'm not very good at dancing.	**Wǒ tiào de bú tài hǎo.** 我跳得不太好。
I'm not very good at swimming.	**Wǒ yóu de bú tài hǎo.** 我游得不太好。

3.7 Paying a compliment

You look great! (to a male)	[formal] **Nǐ kàn shàngqu zhēn shuài!** 你看上去真帅!
	[informal] **Jīntiān zěnme zhème shuài!** 今天怎么这么帅!
I like your car!	**Wǒ xǐhuan nǐde chē!** 我喜欢你的车!
You are very nice.	[formal] **Nǐ (duì) rén zhēn hǎo.** 你(对)人真好。
	[informal] **Nǐ zhēn hǎo.** 你真好。
What a good boy/girl!	**Hǎo háizi!** 好孩子!
You're a good dancer.	**Nǐ tiàowǔ tiàode hěn hǎo.** 你跳舞跳得很好。
You're a very good cook.	**Nǐ zuòcài zuòde hěn hǎo.** 你做菜做得很好。
You're a good soccer player.	**Nǐ zúqiú tīde hěn hǎo.** 你足球踢得很好。

3.8 Intimate comments/questions

I like being with you. **Wǒ xǐhuan gēn nǐ zài yìqǐ.**
我喜欢跟你在一起。

I've missed you so much. **Wǒ fēicháng xiǎngniàn nǐ.**
我非常想念你。

I dreamt about you. **Wǒ mèngjiàn nǐ.** 我梦见你。

I think about you all day. **Wǒ yìtiāndàowǎn dōu xiǎngzhe nǐ.**
我一天到晚都想着你。

I've been thinking about you all day. **Wǒ zhěngtiān dōu zài xiǎng nǐ.**
我整天都在想你。

You have such a sweet smile. **Nǐde xiàoróng zhēn tián.**
你的笑容真甜。

You have such beautiful eyes. **Nǐde yǎnjing zhēn mírén.**
你的眼睛真迷人。

I like (I'm fond of) you. **Wǒ xǐhuanshàng nǐ le.** 我喜欢上你了。

I'm in love with you. **Wǒ àishàng nǐ le.** 我爱上你了。

I'm in love with you too. **Wǒ yě àishàng nǐ le.** 我也爱上你了。

I love you. **Wǒ ài nǐ.** 我爱你。

I love you too. **Wǒ yě ài nǐ.** 我也爱你。

I don't feel as strongly about you. **Wǒ duì nǐ méiyǒu tèbié de gǎnqíng.**
我对你没有特别的感情。

I already have a girlfriend. **Wǒ yǐjīng yǒu nǚpéngyou le.**
我已经有女朋友了。

I already have a boyfriend. **Wǒ yǐjīng yǒu nánpéngyou le.**
我已经有男朋友了。

I'm not ready for that. **Wǒde gǎnqíng hái méiyǒu dào zhè yí bù.** 我的感情还没有到这一步。

I don't want to rush into it.	**Wǒ bù xiǎng zhème kuài jiù xiànjìnqu.** 我不想这么快就陷进去。
Take your hands off me.	**Bǎ nǐde shǒu nákāi!** 把你的手拿开！
Okay, no problem.	**Hǎo, méi wèntí.** 好，没问题。
Will you spend the night with me?	**Nǐ yuànbuyuànyì péi wǒ yì wǎn?** 你愿不愿意陪我一晚？
I'd like to sleep with you.	**Wǒ xiǎng hé nǐ shàng chuáng.** 我想和你上床。
Only if we use a condom.	**Hǎo, búguò wǒmen yídìng yào yòng bìyùntào.** 好，不过我们一定要用避孕套。
We have to be careful about AIDS.	**Wǒmen yào dāngxīn āizībìng.** 我们要当心艾滋病。
We shouldn't take any risks.	**Wǒmen bù yīnggāi mào zhè ge xiǎn.** 我们不应该冒这个险。
Do you have a condom?	**Nǐ yǒu bìyùntào ma?** 你有避孕套吗？
No? Then the answer's no.	**Méiyǒu? Nà, bùxíng.** 没有？那，不行。

3.10 Congratulations and condolences

(Wishing you a) Happy New Year!	**(Zhù nǐ) xīnnián kuàilè!** (祝你)新年快乐！
(Wishing you a) Happy birthday!	**(Zhù nǐ) shēngrì kuàilè!** (祝你)生日快乐！
Please accept my condolences.	**Qǐng jiēshòu wǒde diàoyàn.** 请接受我的吊唁。
My deepest sympathy.	**Wǒ shēn yǒu tónggǎn.** 我深有同感。

3.10 Arrangements

When will I see you again?	**Wǒmen shénme shíhou zài jiànmiàn?** 我们什么时候再见面？
Are you free over the weekend?	**Nǐ zhè ge zhǒumò yǒu méiyǒu kòngr?** 你这个周末有没有空儿？
What's the plan, then?	**Nǐ yǒu shénme ānpái?** 你有什么安排？
Where shall we meet?	**Wǒmen zài nǎr jiànmiàn?** 我们在哪儿见面？
Will you pick me/us up?	**Nǐ kěyǐ lái jiē wǒ/wǒmen ma?** 你可以来接我／我们吗？
Shall I pick you up? [formal]	**Wǒ lái jiē nǐ/nǐmen, hǎo bu hǎo?** 我来接你／你们，好不好？
I have to be home by...	**Wǒ...yǐqián yídìng yào huídào jiālǐ** 我…以前一定要回到家里
I don't want to see you anymore. [formal]	**Wǒ bù xiǎng zài jiàndào nǐ.** 我不想再见到你。

3.11 Being the host(ess)

See also 4 Eating out

What would you like to drink?	[formal] **Nín xiǎng hē shénme yǐnliào?** 您想喝什么饮料？
	[informal] **Xiǎng hē diǎn shénme?** 想喝点什么？
Something non-alcoholic, please.	**Yǒu méiyǒu bù hán jiǔjīng de yǐnliào?** 有没有不含酒精的饮料？
Would you like a cigarette/cigar?	**Xiǎng chōu zhī yān/xuějiā ma?** 想抽只烟／雪茄吗？
I don't smoke.	**(Xièxie) wǒ bù chōuyān.** （谢谢），我不抽烟。

3.12 Saying goodbye

Can I send you home?
[formal]
Wǒ kěyǐ sòng nǐ huíjiā ma?
我可以送你回家吗？

Can I email/call you?
Wǒ kěyǐ gěi nǐ fā diànzǐ yóujiàn/dǎ diànhuà ma?
我可以给你发电子邮件／打电话吗？

Will you text me/call me?
Nǐ kěyǐ gěi wǒ fā duǎnxìn/dǎ diànhuà ma? 你可以给我发短信／打电话吗？

Can I have your mobile number/email address?
Wǒ kěyǐ yào nǐde shǒujī hàomǎ/ diànzǐ yóujiàn dìzhǐ ma?
我可以要你的手机号码／电子邮件
地址吗？

Thanks for everything.
Gǎnxiè nǐ wèi wǒ zuò de yíqiè.
感谢你为我做的一切。

It was a lot of fun.
Wánrde hěn kāixīn. 玩儿得很开心。

Send my regards to...
[informal]
Qǐng dài wǒ gēn...wènhòu
请代我跟…问候

All the best!
Wànshì-rúyì! 万事如意！

Good luck.
Zhù nǐ hǎo yùn. 祝你好运。

When will you be back?
[informal]
Nǐ shénme shíhou huílai?
你什么时候回来？

I'll be waiting for you.
Wǒ huì děng nǐ huílai. 我会等你回来。

I'd like to see you again.
Wǒ xiǎng zài jiàndào nǐ.
我想再见到你。

I hope we meet again soon.
Wǒ xiǎng hěn kuài zài jiàndào nǐ.
我想很快再见到你。

Here's my address if you're ever in the United States.
Zhè shì wǒde dìzhǐ. Yǒu yìtiān nǐ dào Měiguó lái, yídìng yào lái zhǎo wǒ.
这是我的地址。有一天你到美国来，
一定要来找我。

4. Eating Out

Foreigners visiting China have a wide range of cuisines to choose from, such as Peking Duck, Sichuan hotpot, Mongolian barbecues and Shanghai dumplings. You may have to make reservations at some restaurants outside the hotels. Most restaurants provide complimentary Chinese tea. In China people usually have three meals:

1. **zǎofàn** 早饭 (breakfast) is eaten sometime between 7.30 and 10 a.m. It generally consists of buns, congee, eggs, assorted pickles and noodles.

2. **wǔfàn** 午饭 (lunch) is traditionally eaten at home between 12 noon and 2 p.m. Some schoolchildren return home, while others eat their packed lunch in school. Lunch usually comprises rice, a main course of meat or fish with a range of vegetable dishes, or noodles with meat and vegetables.

3. **wǎnfàn** 晚饭 (dinner) is considered to be the most important meal of the day, at around 7 or 8 p.m. It often includes rice, a soup and a few meat and vegetable dishes, and is usually taken with the family.

4.1 At the restaurant

I'd like to reserve a table for seven o'clock, please.

Wǒ xiǎng dìng yì zhāng zhuō, dìng zài qīdiǎn. 我想订一张桌，订在七点。

| A table for two, please. | **Wǒ xiǎng dìng yì zhāng liǎng ge rén de zhuō.** 我想订一张两个人的桌。 |

| We've reserved. | **Wǒmen yùdìng le.** 我们预订了。 |

| We haven't reserved. | **Wǒmen hái méi yùdìng.** 我们还没预订。 |

请稍等！ **Qǐng shāo děng!**	A moment, please.
你预订座位了没有？ **Nǐ yùdìng zuòwèile méiyǒu?**	Do you have a reservation?
你们用谁的名字预订的？ **Nǐmen yòng shuí de míngzi yùdìng de?**	What name please?
这边请。 **Zhè biān qǐng.**	This way, please.
对不起，这张桌已经预订了。 **Duìbuqǐ, zhè zhāng zhuō yǐjīng yùdìngle.**	Sorry, this table is reserved.
十五分钟以后有一张空桌子。 **Shíwǔ fēnzhōng yǐhòu yǒu yì zhāng kōng zhuōzi.**	We'll have a table free in fifteen minutes.

| Would you mind waiting? | **Nǐ jiè bu jiéyí děngyiděng?** 你介不介意等一等？ |

| Is the restaurant open yet? | **Cāntīng kāimén le méiyǒu?** 餐厅开门了没有？ |

| What time does the restaurant open? | **Cāntīng shénme shíhou kāimén?** 餐厅什么时候开门？ |

| What time does the restaurant close? | **Cāntīng shénme shíhou guānmén?** 餐厅什么时候关门？ |

| Can we wait for a table? | **Yàoshi/Rúguǒ wǒmen děng yíxià, yǒu méiyǒu zhuōzi?** 要是／如果我们等一下，有没有桌子？ |

| Do we have to wait long? | **Wǒmen děi děng hěn jiǔ ma?** 我们得等很久吗？ |

Is this seat taken?	**Zhè ge wèizi yǒurén zuò ma?** 这个位子有人坐吗？
Could we sit here/there?	**Wǒmen kěyǐ zuò zài zhèr/nàr ma?** 我们可以坐在这儿／那儿吗？
Can we sit by the window?	**Wǒmen kěyǐ kào chuānghu zuò ma?** 我们可以靠窗户坐吗？
Are there any tables outside?	**Wàibiān yǒu méiyǒu kōng zhuōzi?** 外边有没有空桌子？
Do you have another chair for us?	**Gěi wǒmen zài ná yì bǎ yǐzi, hǎo ma?** 给我们再拿一把椅子，好吗？
Do you have a high chair?	**Yǒu méiyǒu gěi xiǎo háizi zuò de gāo yǐzi?** 有没有给小孩子坐的高椅子？
Is there a socket for this bottle-warmer?	**Yǒu méiyǒu chā zhè ge nuǎnpíngqì de chāzuó?** 有没有插这个暖瓶器的插座？
Could you warm up this bottle for me?	**Qǐng gěi wǒ nuǎn yíxià zhè ge nǎipíng.** 请给我暖一下这个奶瓶。
Could you warm up this jar (in the microwave) for me?	**Qǐng gěi wǒ (zài wéibōlú lǐ) nuǎn yíxià zhè ge dàkǒupíng.** 请给我(在微波炉里)暖一下这个大口瓶。
Not too hot, please.	**Qǐng búyào tài tàng.** 请不要太烫。
Is there somewhere I can change the baby's diaper?	**Yǒu méiyǒu dìfang gěi yīng'ér huàn niàobù?** 有没有地方给婴儿换尿布？
Where are the restrooms?	**Cèsuǒ zài nǎr?** 厕所在哪儿？

4.1 Ordering

Waiter/Waitress!	**Fúwù yuán!** 服务员！
Madam!	**Nǚshì!** 女士！
Sir!	**Xiānsheng!** 先生！

We'd like something to eat.	**Wǒmen xiǎng chī diǎn dōngxi.** 我们想吃点东西。
We'd like something to drink.	**Wǒmen xiǎng hē diǎn dōngxi.** 我们想喝点东西。
Could I have a quick meal?	**Yǒu méiyǒu kuàicān?** 有没有快餐？
We don't have much time.	**Wǒmen shíjiān bù duō.** 我们时间不多。
We'd like to have a drink first.	**Wǒmen xiǎng xiān hē yǐnliào.** 我们想先喝饮料。
Could we see the menu, please?	**Qǐng gěi wǒmen kànkan càidān.** 请给我们看看菜单。
Could we see the wine list, please?	**Qǐng gěi wǒmen kànkan jiǔdān.** 请给我们看看酒单。
Do you have an English menu?	**Yǒu méiyǒu Yīngwén de càidān?** 有没有英文的菜单？
Do you have a dish of the day?	**Jīntiān yǒu méiyǒu tèbié de cài?** 今天有没有特别的菜？
Do you have a tourist menu?	**Yǒu méiyǒu zhuānmén gěi lǚkè yòng de càidān?** 有没有专门给旅客用的菜单？
We haven't made a choice yet.	**Wǒmen hái méi xiǎnghǎo jiào shénme cài.** 我们还没想好叫什么菜。
What do you recommend?	**Nǐ kěyǐ gěi wǒmen jièshào jǐ dào cài ma?** 你可以给我们介绍几道菜吗？
What are the local specialities?	**Nǐmen běndì yǒu shénme tèsè?** 你们本地有什么特色？
What are your specialities?	**Nǐmen fàn'guǎn tuījiàn shénme tèsè de cài?** 你们饭馆推荐什么特色的菜？
I like chilli.	**Wǒ xǐhuan làjiāo.** 我喜欢辣椒。
I like preserved vegetables.	**Wǒ xǐhuan pàocài.** 我喜欢泡菜。

I don't like meat. **Wǒ bù xǐhuan chī ròu.** 我不喜欢吃肉。

I don't like fish. **Wǒ bù xǐhuan chī yú.** 我不喜欢吃鱼。

What's this? **Zhè shì shénme?** 这是什么？

Does it have...in it? **Lǐmiàn yǒu méiyǒu...?** 里面有没有…？

Is it stuffed with...? **Lǐmiàn bāo de shìbushì...?** 里面包的是不是…？

What does it taste like? **Chīqǐlai shénme wèi?** 吃起来什么味？

Is this a hot or cold dish? **Zhè dào cài shì rè de háishi liáng de?** 这道菜是热的还是凉的？

Is this sweet? **Zhè ge tián ma?** 这个甜吗？

Is this spicy? **Zhè ge là ma?** 这个辣吗？

Do you have anything else, by any chance? **Nǐmen hái yǒu xiē bié de cài ma?** 你们还有别的菜吗？

I'm on a salt-free diet. **Wǒ bù chī yán.** 我不吃盐。

I can't eat pork. **Wǒ bù néng chī zhūròu.** 我不能吃猪肉。

您/你们要什么？
Nín/nǐmen yào shénme?
What would you like?

要点菜了吗？
Yàodiǎn càile ma?
Have you decided?

要不要先来杯饮料？
Yàobuyào xiān lái bēi yǐnliào?
Would you like a drink first?

喝点什么？
Hē diǎn shénme?
What would you like to drink?

我们刚卖完…
Wǒmen gāng mài wán...
We've run out of...

菜来了，请用吧。
Cài láile, qǐng yòng ba.
Enjoy your meal.

饭菜做得怎么样?
Fàncài zuò de zěnmeyàng?

Is everything all right?

我可以收盘子了吗?
Wǒ kěyǐ shōupánzi le ma?

May I clear the table?

I can't have sugar.

Wǒ bù néng chī táng. 我不能吃糖。

I'm on a fat-free diet.

Wǒ bù chī gāozhīfáng de shíwù.
我不吃高脂肪的食物。

I can't have spicy food.

Wǒ bù néng chī là de dōngxi.
我不能吃辣的东西。

We'll have what those
   people are having.

Wǒmen yào tāmen chī de nàzhǒng.
我们要他们吃的那种。

I'd like...

Lái yí ge... 来一个…

We're not having
   Peking Duck.

Wǒmen bù chī Běijīng Kǎoyā.
我们不吃北京烤鸭。

Could I have some
   more rice, please?

Zài gěi wǒ lái diǎnr mǐfàn.
再给我来点儿米饭。

Could I have a glass of
   drinking water, please?

Qǐng gěi wǒ yí bēi báikāishuǐ.
请给我一杯白开水。

Could I have another bottle
of drinking water, please?

Zài gěi wǒ yì píng báikāishuǐ.
再给我一瓶白开水。

Could I have another
   bottle of wine please?

Zài gěi wǒ yì píng jiǔ.
再给我一瓶酒。

Could I have another
   portion of..., please?

Qǐng zài gěi wǒ yí fèn....
请再给我一份…

Could I have the salt
   and pepper, please?

Qǐng gěi wǒ yán hé hújiāo.
请给我盐和胡椒。

Could I have a napkin,
   please?

Qǐng gěi wǒ yī zhāng cānján.
请给我一张餐巾。

Could I have a teaspoon,
   please?

Qǐng gěi wǒ yí ge cháchí.
请给我一个茶匙。

Could I have an ashtray, please? **Qǐng gěi wǒ yí ge yānhuīgāng.** 请给我一个烟灰缸。

Could I have some toothpicks, please? **Qǐng gěi wǒ jǐ gēn yáqiān.** 请给我几根牙签。

Could I have a straw please? **Qǐng gěi wǒ yì gēn xīguǎn.** 请给我一根吸管。

Cheers! **Gānbēi!** 干杯！

The next round's on me. **Xiàcì wǒ qǐngkè.** 下次我请客。

Could we have a doggy bag, please? **Qǐng gěi wǒmen dǎbāo.** 请给我们打包。

 The bill

See also 8.2 Settling the bill

How much is this dish? **Zhè pán cài duōshao qián?** 这盘菜多少钱？

Could I have the bill, please? **Qǐng gěi wǒ zhàngdān.** 请给我账单。

All together. **Yígòng....** 一共…

Everyone pays separately. **Wǒmen gè fù gè de zhàngdān ba.** 我们各付各的账单吧。

Let's go Dutch. **Zánmen píngtān zhàngdān ba.** 咱们平摊账单吧。

Could we have the menu again, please? **Qǐng zài gěi wǒmen càidān kànkan.** 请再给我们菜单看看。

The...is not on the bill. **Zhàngdān shàng méiyǒu zhè ge...** 账单上没有这个…

 Complaints

It's taking a very long time. **Wǒ yǐjīng děngle hěn jiǔ le.** 我已经等了很久了。

This must be a mistake. | **Wǒ kàn nǐmen gǎocuò le.**
我看你们搞错了。

This is not what I ordered. | **Zhè bú shì wǒ diǎn de cài.**
这不是我点的菜。

I ordered... | **Wǒ yào de shì...** 我要的是…

There's a dish missing. | **Hái chà yí ge cài.** 还差一个菜。

The plate is broken. | **Zhè ge pán quēkǒule.** 这个盘缺口了。

The plate is not clean. | **Zhè ge pán bù gānjìng.** 这个盘不干净。

The food's cold. | **Zhè pán cài lěngle.** 这盘菜冷了。

The food's not fresh. | **Zhè pán cài bù xīnxiān le.**
这盘菜不新鲜了。

The food has gone bad. | **Zhè pán cài huài le.** 这盘菜坏了。

The food's too salty. | **Zhè pán cài tài xián le.**
这盘菜太咸了。

The food's too sweet. | **Zhè pán cài tài tián le.**
这盘菜太甜了。

The food's too spicy. | **Zhè pán cài tài là le.** 这盘菜太辣了。

Could I have something else instead of this? | **Qǐng gěi wǒ huàn biéde cài.**
请给我换别的菜。

The bill/this amount is not right. | **Zhàngdān suànde bú duì.**
账单算得不对。

We didn't have this. | **Wǒmen méiyǒu yào zhè ge cài.**
我们没有要这个菜。

There's no toilet paper in the restroom. | **Xǐshǒujiān lǐ méiyǒu wèishēngzhǐ le.**
洗手间没有卫生纸了。

Will you call the manager, please? | **Qǐng jiào nǐmende jīnglǐ lái.**
请叫你们的经理来。

4.5 Paying a compliment

That was a sumptuous meal.	**Fàncài hěn fēngshèng.** 饭菜很丰盛。
The food was excellent.	**Fàncài hǎojíle.** 饭菜好极了。
The...in particular was delicious.	**Tèbié shì..., tài hǎochī le.** 特别是…，太好吃了。

4.6 Requests

Please give me the menu.	**Qǐng gěi wǒ càidān.** 请给我菜单。
a pair of chopsticks	**yì shuāng kuàzi** 一双筷子
a fork	**yì bǎ cānchā/chāzi** 一把餐叉／叉子
a knife	**yì bǎ dāozi** 一把刀
a plate	**yí ge pánzi** 一个盘子
a bowl	**yí ge wǎn** 一个碗
a spoon	**yì bǎ tāngchí** 一把汤匙
a ladle	**yì bǎ sháozi/tāngsháo** 一把勺子／汤勺
salt	**yán** 盐
pepper	**hújiāo** 胡椒
sugar	**táng** 糖
fruit	**shuǐguǒ** 水果
ice cream	**bīngjīlíng/bīngqílín** 冰激凌/冰淇淋
meat	**ròu (shí)** 肉(食)
salad	**shālā** 沙拉
main course	**zhǔcài** 主菜
side dishes/vegetables	**pèicài/shūcài** 配菜/蔬菜
service charge	**fúwùfèi** 服务费
included	**yǐ bāokuò zài nèi** 已包括在内

soup	**tāng** 汤
specialities	**tèsècài** 特色菜
snacks	**xiāochī** 小吃
bread	**miànbāo** 面包
cakes/desserts	**dàn gāo/tiánshí** 蛋糕/甜食
noodles	**miàntiáo** 面条
vegetables	**shūcài** 蔬菜
fish	**yú** 鱼

4.7 Drinks

hot cocoa	**rè kěkě** 热可可
cold milk	**lěng niúnǎi** 冷牛奶
black tea	**hóngchá (bù jiā nǎi)** 红茶(不加奶)
milk tea	**nǎichá** 奶茶
coffee	**kāfēi** 咖啡
jasmine tea	**mòlì huāchá** 茉莉花茶
beer	**píjiǔ** 啤酒
orange juice	**júzizhī/liǔdīngzhī** 桔子汁／柳丁汁
mineral water	**kuàng quánshuǐ** 矿泉水
soda water	**sūdǎshuǐ** 苏打水
Coca Cola	**kěkǒu kělè** 可口可乐
brandy	**báilándì** 白兰地
whisky	**wēishìjì** 威士忌
champagne	**xiāngbīnjiǔ** 香槟酒
red wine	**hóng pútaojiǔ/hóngjiǔ** 红葡萄酒／红酒
white wine	**bái pútaojiǔ** 白葡萄酒

 **The menu**

Chinese dishes	**Zhōngcān** 中餐
assorted cold dishes	**lěng pīnpán/liángcài** 冷拼盘／凉菜
pickled cabbage	**pàocài** 泡菜
sautéd chicken with chili pepper and peanuts	**jiàngbào jīdīng** 酱爆鸡丁
fish with sweet and sour sauce	**tángcù yú** 糖醋鱼
sautéd fried prawns	**zhá pēng xiāduàn** 炸烹虾段
sweet and sour pork	**gǔlǎoròu** 咕唠肉
sautéd mutton sliced with scallions	**cōngbào yángròu** 葱爆羊肉
sautéd beef with onion	**yángcōng chǎo niúròu** 洋葱炒牛肉
sautéd mushroom and choy sum	**xiānggū càixīn** 香菇菜心
sautéd beancurd with brown sauce	**hóngshāo dòufu** 红烧豆腐
steamed rice	**mǐfàn** 米饭
fried rice with eggs	**dàn chǎofàn** 鸡蛋炒饭
Western dishes	**Xīcān** 西餐
soft boiled egg	**zhǔ jīdàn** 煮鸡蛋
scrambled egg	**chǎo jīdàn** 炒鸡蛋
toast	**kǎo miànbāo piàn** 烤面包片
sandwich	**sānmíngzhì** 三明治
butter	**huángyóu** 黄油
cheese	**nǎilào/rǔlào** 奶酪／乳酪
jam	**guǒjiàng** 果酱
pizza	**bǐsābǐng** 比萨饼

Eating Out

4

5. Getting Around

 5.1 Asking directions

Excuse me, could I ask you something?	**Láojià, wǒ kěyǐ wèn nín yíxià ma?** 劳驾，我可以问您一下吗？
I've lost my way.	**Wǒ mílù le.** 我迷路了。
Is there a ... around here?	**Fùjìn yǒu méiyǒu...?** 附近有没有⋯？
Excuse me, what direction is ...?	**Qǐngwèn, ...zài nǎ ge fāngxiàng?** 请问，⋯在哪个方向？
Excuse me, am I going the right way to get to the bus stop?	**Qǐngwèn, gōnggòng qìchēzhàn zǒu zhè ge fāngxiàng duì ma?** 请问，公共汽车站走这个方向对吗？
Excuse me, is this the right direction to the railway station?	**Qǐngwèn, huǒchēzhàn zǒu zhè ge fāngxiàng duì ma?** 请问，火车站走这个方向对吗？
Could you tell me how to get to...?	**Qǐngwèn, ...zěnme zǒu?** 请问，⋯怎么走？
How many kilometers is it to...?	**Dào...yǒu duōshao gōnglǐ?** 到⋯有多少公里？
Is it far?	**Yuǎn bu yuǎn?** 远不远？

Can I walk there? **Kěyǐ zǒulù qù ma?** 可以走路去吗?

Is it difficult to find? **Hǎo bu hǎo zhǎo?** 好不好找?

我不请楚，我不认识这里的路。
Wǒ bù qǐngchu, wǒ bú rènshi zhèlǐ de lù.
I don't know, I don't know my way around here.

你走错了。
Nǐ zǒu cuòle.
You're going the wrong way.

你要往回走。
Nǐ yào wǎng huí zǒu.
You have to go back.

从那儿开始，跟着路牌走。
Cóng nàr kāishǐ, gēnzhe lùpái zǒu.
From there on just follow the signs.

到那边再问。
Dào nàbiān zài wèn.
When you get there, ask again.

一直走下去。
Yīzhí zǒu xiàqù.
Go straight ahead.

过
Guò
Cross

转右
Zhuǎnyòu
Turn right

转左。
Zhuǎnzuǒ.
Turn left

顺着／沿着
shùnzhe/yánzhe
Follow

road/street
lù/jiē
路／街

overpass
gāojiàqiáo
高架桥

the building
lóufáng
楼房

river
hé
河

tunnel
suìdào
隧道

at the corner
jiējiǎo/guǎijiǎo (jiǎoluò)
街角／拐角〔角落〕

traffic light
hónglǜdēng/jiāotōngdēng
红绿灯／交通灯

bridge
qiáo
桥

arrow sign
jiàntóu biāozhì
箭头标志

5.2 Traffic signs

交通标志
Jiāotōng Biāozhì
Traffic Signs

十字路口
Shízìlùkǒu
Intersection/
Crossroads

汽车故障服务处
**Qìchē Gùzhàng
Fúwùchù**
Road Assistance
(Breakdown
Service)

停(车)
Tíng (Chē)
Stop (Vehicle)

限时停车
Xiànshí Tíngchē
Parking For a
Limited Period

加油站
Jiāyóuzhàn
Service Station

不准堵塞
Bùzhǔn Dǔsè
Do Not Obstruct

路面损坏／不平
**Lùmiàn Sǔnhuài/
Bùpíng**
Broken/Uneven
Surface

当心
Dāngxīn
Beware

需用雪链
Xūyòng Xuěliàn
Snow Chains
Required

前面路窄
Qiánmiàn Lùzhǎi
Narrowing in the Road

交通道／人行道
Jiāotōngdào/Rénxíngdào
Traffic Island/Pedestrian Walk

进隧道请开前灯
Jìn Suìdào Qǐng Kāi Qiándēng
Turn On Headlights (in the
Tunnel)

收费停车／专用车位
**Shōufèi Tíngchē/Zhuānyòng
Chēwèi**
Paying Carpark/
Parking Reserved For

靠右行／靠左行
Kào Yòu Xíng/Kào Zuǒ Xíng
Keep Right/Left

当心山上石头
Dāngxīn Shānshàng Shítou
Beware of Falling Rocks

监控车库／停车场
Jiānkòng Chēkù/Tíngchēchǎng
Supervised Garage/Parking Lot

(必须显示)停放车标
**(Bìxū Xiǎnshì) Tíngfàng Chē
Biāo**
Parking Disk (Compulsory)

(铁路公路)交叉口
(Tiělù Gōnglù) Jiāochākǒu
Grade Crossing

下一段路多雨或雪
Xià Yíduàn Lù Duōyǔ Huò Xuě
Rain or Ice For...kms

停车被拖走地带
Tíngchē Bèi Tuōzǒu Dìdài
Tow-Away Area (Both Sides of
the Road)

绕道
Ràodào
Detour

道路阻塞
Dàolù Zǔsè
Road Blocked

换行车道
**Huànxíng
Chēdào**
Change Lanes

道路封闭
Dàolù Fēngbì
Road Closed

出口
Chūkǒu
Exit

紧急行车道
Jǐnjí Xíngchēdào
Emergency
Lane

车道
Chēdào
Driveway

急转弯
Jízhuǎnwān
Curves

不准驶入
Bùzhǔn Shǐrù
No Entry

慢行
Mànxíng
Slow Down

(交通) 环岛
**(Jiāotōng)
Huándǎo**
Traffic Circle
(Roundabout)

前面修路 **Qiánmiàn Xiūlù** Roadworks Ahead	先使用车道权 **Xiān Shǐyòng Chēdàoquán** Right of Way	不准超车 **Bù Zhǔn Chāochē** No Passing
路不开放 **Lù Bù Kāifàng** Road Closed	不准搭乘他人便车 **Bù Zhǔn Dāchéng Tārén Biànchē** No Hitchhiking	不准停车 **Bù Zhǔn Tíngchē** No Parking
载重卡车 **Zàizhòng Kǎchē** Heavy Trucks	不准转右／左 **Bù Zhǔn Zhuǎnyòu/Zuǒ** No Right/Left Turn	单行道 **Dānxíng Dào** One Way
净空高度 **Jìngkōng Gāodù** Maximum Height	先使用车道权在路尾 **Xiān Shǐyòng Chēdàoquán Zài Lùwěi** Right of Way at End of Road	隧道 **Suìdào** Tunnel
最高速度 **Zuìgāo Sùdù** Maximum Speed		通行费 **Tōngxíng Fèi** Toll Payment

 The car

See the diagram on page 75

The speed limits for vehicles vary in different cities and on different roads. Generally speaking, the speed limit for cars is 110 km/h on expressways, 80 km/h on main roads and 70 km/h in built-up areas. For motorcycles the limits are 60 km/h on main roads, 50 km/h in built-up areas. Motorcycles are not allowed to travel on expressways.

It's recommended to hire a driver while in China, rather than navigating the roads in a rental car. If you do decide to drive, however, you'll need a provisional driver's licence that you could get from places like Beijing International Airport. Bring the completed application form, three colored passport-sized photographs, your driver's licence, international driving permit (and its Chinese translations) as well as your hotel booking voucher. The length of time you're allowed to drive in China depends also on the visa that you get.

The parts of a car

(the diagram shows the numbered parts)

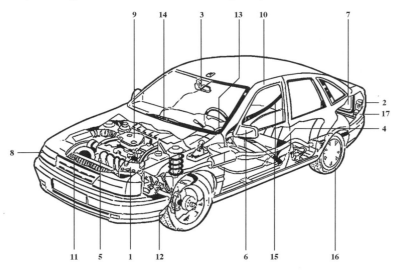

	backup light	**hòubǔdēng**	后补灯
	fuel pump	**rányóubèng**	燃油泵
	fan	**gǔfēngqì**	鼓风器
1	battery	**diànchí**	电池
2	rear light	**hòudēng**	后灯
3	rear-view mirror	**hòushìjìng**	后视镜
4	gas tank	**yóuxiāng**	油箱
5	spark plugs	**huǒhuāsāi**	火花塞
6	side mirror	**cèshìjìng**	侧视镜
7	trunk	**chēwěixiāng**	车尾箱
8	headlight	**qiándēng**	前灯
9	air filter	**guòlǜqì**	过滤器
10	door	**chēmén**	车门
11	radiator	**shuǐxiāng**	水箱
12	brake disc	**shāchēdié**	刹车碟
13	indicator	**zhǐshìqì**	指示器
14	windshield wiper	**dǎngfēng bōli yǔshuā**	挡风玻璃雨刷
15	seat belt	**ānquándài**	安全带
16	wheel	**chēlún**	车轮
17	spare wheel	**bèiyòng lún**	备用轮

5.4 The gas station

How many kilometers to the next gas station, please?	**Qǐng wèn, dào xià yí ge jiāyóuzhàn yǒu duō yuǎn?** 请问，到下一个加油站有多远？
I would like 50 liters of unleaded #93.	**Wǒ yào wǔshí gōngshēng jiǔshísānhào wúqiān qìyóu.** 我要五十公升九十三号无铅汽油。
I would like 50 liters of unleaded #90.	**Wǒ yào wǔshí gōngshēng jiǔshíhào wúqiān qìyóu.** 我要五十公升九十号无铅汽油。
I would like 50 liters of leaded petrol.	**Wǒ yào wǔshí gōngshēng hánqiān qìyóu.** 我要五十公升含铅汽油。
I would like 50 liters of diesel.	**Wǒ yào wǔshí gōngshēng cháiyóu.** 我要五十公升柴油。
I would like 50 dollars worth of gas.	**Wǒ yào wǔshí yuán de qìyóu.** 我要五十元的汽油。
Fill her up, please.	**Qǐng jiāmǎn yóuxiāng.** 请加满油箱。
Could you check the oil level?	**Qǐng gěi wǒ jiǎnchá jīyóu gòu bu gòu mǎn?** 请给我检查机油够不够满？
Could you check the tire pressure?	**Qǐng gěi wǒ lúntāi qì gòu bu gòu mǎn?** 请给我检查轮胎气够不够满？
Could you change the oil, please?	**Qǐng gěi wǒ huàn jīyóu.** 请给我换机油。
Could you clean the windshield, please?	**Qǐng gěi wǒ cāyicā dǎngfēng bōli.** 请给我擦一擦挡风玻璃。
Could you wash the car, please?	**Qǐng gěi wǒ xǐ chē.** 请给我洗车。

5.5 Breakdowns and repairs

My car has broken down, could you give me a hand?	**Wǒde chē huàile, nǐ néng bāngzhu wǒ ma?** 我的车坏了, 你能帮助我吗?
I have run out of gas.	**Wǒde chē méiyǒu qìyóu le.** 我的车没有汽油了。
I've locked the keys in the car.	**Wǒ bǎ yàoshi suǒ zài chē lǐmiàn le.** 我把钥匙锁在车里面了。
The car won't start.	**Wǒde qìchè bù néng qǐdòng.** 我的汽车不能起动。
The motorbike won't start.	**Wǒde mótuōchē bù néng qǐdòng.** 我的摩托车不能起动。
Could you contact the breakdown service for me, please?	**Qǐng gěi wǒ liánluò gùzhàng fúwùchù.** 请给我联络故障服务处。
Could you call a garage for me, please?	**Qǐng gěi wǒ jiào xiūchēchǎng.** 请给我叫修车厂。
Could you give me a lift to the nearest garage?	**Nǐ kě bu kěyǐ dài wǒ dào zuìjìn de xiūchēchǎng ?** 你可不可以带我到最近的修车厂?
Could you give me a lift to the nearest town?	**Nǐ kě bu kěyǐ dài wǒ dào zuìjìn de xiāngzhèn?** 你可不可以带我到最近的乡镇?
Could you give me a lift to the nearest phone booth?	**Nǐ kě bu kěyǐ dài wǒ dào zuìjìn de gōngyòng diànhuà?** 你可不可以带我到最近的公用电话?
Could you take me to the nearest emergency phone?	**Nǐ kě bu kěyǐ dài wǒ dào zuìjìn de jǐnjí diànhuà?** 你可不可以带我到最近的紧急电话?
Can we take my motorcycle?	**Nǐ kěyǐ yùn wǒde mótuōchē ma?** 你可以运我的摩托车吗?

Could you tow me to a garage?	**Kěyǐ tuō wǒde chē dào xiūchēchǎng ma?** 可以拖我的车到修车厂吗？
There's probably something wrong with...	**....kěnéng yǒu máobìng** …可能有毛病
Can you fix it?	**Kěyǐ xiūlǐ ma?** 可以修理吗？
Could you fix my tire?	**Kěyǐ bǔ lúntāi ma?** 可以补轮胎吗？
Could you change this wheel?	**Kěyǐ gěi wǒ huàn zhè ge lúntāi ma?** 可以给我换这个轮胎吗？
Can you fix it so it'll get me to...?	**Kěyǐ gěi wǒ xiūyixiū, ràng wǒ néng kāidào...** 可以给我修一修，让我能开到…
Which garage can help me?	**Nǎ yì jiā xiūchēchǎng néng bāngzhu wǒ?** 哪一家修车厂能帮助我？
When will my car be ready?	**Wǒde qìchē shénme shíhou néng xiūhǎo?** 我的汽车什么时候能修好？
When will my bicycle be ready?	**Wǒde zìxíngchē shénme shíhou néng xiūhǎo?** 我的自行车什么时候能修好？
Have you already finished?	**Nǐ gěi wǒ xiūhǎo le méiyǒu?** 你给我修好了没有？
Can I wait for it here?	**Wǒ kěyǐ zài zhèr děng nǐ xiūhǎo ma?** 我可以在这儿等你修好吗？
How much will it cost?	**Xiūlǐfèi shì duōshao?** 修理费是多少？
Could you itemize the bill?	**Kěyǐ bǎ xiūlǐ de xiàngmù qīngdān gěi wǒ kàn ma?** 可以把修理的项目清单给我看吗？
Please give me a receipt for insurance purposes.	**Qǐng gěi wǒ kāi zhāng fāpiào, wǒ xūyào gěi bǎoxiǎn gōngsī kàn.** 请给我开张发票，我需要给保险公司看。

我没有你要的配件。
Wǒ méiyǒu nǐ yào de pèijiàn.

I don't have parts for your vehicle.

我要去别的地方给你找配件。
Wǒ yào qù bié de dìfāng gěi nǐ zhǎo pèijiàn.

I have to get the parts from somewhere else.

我需要给你订配件。
Wǒ xūyào gěi nǐ dìng pèijiàn.

I have to order the parts.

那需要半天时间。
Nà xūyào bàntiān shíjiān.

That'll take half a day.

那需要一天时间。
Nà xūyào yītiān shíjiān.

That'll take a day.

那需要几天时间。
Nà xūyào jǐtiān shíjiān.

That'll take a few days.

那需要一个星期时间。
Nà xūyào yígè xīngqí shíjiān.

That'll take a week.

修理费超过汽车的价值。
Xiūlǐ fèi chāoguò qìchē de jiàzhí.

Your car is a write-off.

修理费超过自行车的价值。
Xiūlǐ fèi chāoguò zìxíngchē de jiàzhí.

Your bicycle is a write-off.

你的汽车不能修。
Nǐ de qìchē bùnéng xiū.

Your car can't be repaired.

你的摩托车不能修。
Nǐ de mótuōchē bùnéng xiū.

Your motorbike can't be repaired.

你的助动车不能修。
Nǐ de zhùdòngchē bùnéng xiū.

Your moped can't be repaired.

你的自行车不能修。
Nǐ de zìxíngchē bùnéng xiū.

Your bicycle can't be repaired.

你的汽车…点就能修好。
Nǐ de qìchē…diǎn jiù néng xiūhǎo.

The car will be ready at...o'clock.

你的摩托车…点就能修好。
Nǐ de mótuōchē…diǎn jiù néng xiūhǎo.

The motorbike will be ready at ...o'clock.

你的助动车…点就能修好。
Nǐ de zhùdòngchē …diǎn jiù néng xiūhǎo.

The moped will be ready at ...o'clock.

你的自行车…点就能修好。
Nǐ de zìxíngchē … diǎn jiù néng xiūhǎo.

The bicycle will be ready at ...o'clock.

5.6 Bicycles/mopeds

The bicycle is the main means of transport for ordinary citizens in China. There are tens of millions of bicycles in China and you will find that there is at least one bicycle for every family.

Mopeds are mechanized bicycles for longer distance commuting and because of their speed, the wearing of crash helmets is compulsory—same for motorcyclists.

The parts of a bicycle

(the diagram shows the numbered parts)

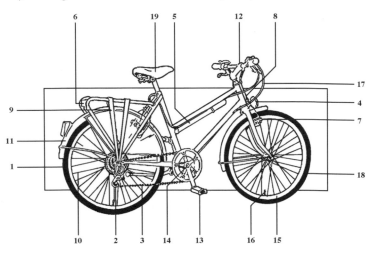

1	rear wheel	**hòulún**	后轮
2	gear change	**biànsùgān**	变速杆
3	chain	**liàndài**	链带
4	headlight	**qiándēng**	前灯
5	pump	**dǎqìtǒng**	打气筒
6	reflector	**fǎnshèjìng**	反射镜
7	brake shoe	**shāchēpiàn**	刹车片
8	brake cable	**shāchēxiàn**	刹车线
9	carrier straps	**yùnzài bùdài**	运载布带
10	spoke	**gāngsī**	钢丝
11	mudguard	**dǎngníbǎn**	挡泥板

12	handlebar	**bǎshǒu**	把手
13	toe clip	**tàbǎnkòu**	踏板扣
14	drum brake	**gǔ shāchē**	鼓刹车
15	valve	**huómén**	活门
16	valve tube	**zhēngkōngguǎn**	真空管
17	gear cable	**biànsùxiàn**	变速线
18	front wheel	**qiánlún**	前轮
19	seat	**zuòwèi**	座位

People rely on bicycles and mopeds to take them to work, do their shopping and for recreational purposes. As China modernizes, bicycles are increasingly barred from highways and ring roads, Mopeds and bicycles are limited to special lanes in urban areas.

In Shanghai and Beijing, a recent ridesharing service, Mobike, has been launched so you can rent a bicycle using your mobile phone. While the app locks your bicycle, be considerate and don't leave it in places that are hard to find. There are also many other rental places around the city, and you'll need a Public Bike Rental Card (for those aged 18-65 only).

5.7 Renting a vehicle

I'd like to rent a car.	**Wǒ xiǎng zū yí liàng chē.** 我想租一辆车。
I'd like to rent a bicycle.	**Wǒ xiǎng zū yí liàng zìxíngchē.** 我想租一辆自行车。
I'd like to rent a small car.	**Wǒ yào zū yí liàng xiǎode chē.** 我要租一辆小的车。
Do I need a (special) license for that?	**Wǒ xūyào (tèbiéde) zhízhào ma?** 我需要（特别的）执照吗？
I'd like to rent it for a day.	**Wǒ xiǎng zū yì tiān.** 我想租一天。
I'd like to rent it for two days.	**Wǒ xiǎng zū liǎng tiān.** 我想租两天。

What is the rental cost per day?	**Zūjīn yì tiān duōshao qián?** 租金一天多少钱?
What is the rental cost per week?	**Zūjīn yì xīngqí duōshao qián?** 租金一星期多少钱?
How much is the deposit?	**Yājīn yào fù duōshao qián?** 押金要付多少钱?
Could I have a receipt for the deposit?	**Qǐng gěi wǒ yājīn shōujù.** 请给我押金收据。
Does that include insurance?	**Shōufèi bāokuò bǎoxiǎnfèi ma?** 收费包括保险费吗?
What time can I pick the car up?	**Wǒ shénme shíhou lái qǔ chē?** 我什么时候来取车?
When does the car have to be back?	**Chē shénme shíhou yào huán?** 车什么时候要还?

5.8 Getting a lift

Hitchhiking in China is usually quite rare, and the ubiquitous "thumbs up" signal would likely be understood as "good" rather than you needing a ride. There are some ways to get a ride, though. First of all, be sure to dress neatly and avoid wearing sunglasses as you could potentially look a little too sinister.

Make a big sign detailing where you want to go in Chinese characters, and provide alternate locations (a mid-way point for example) so as to give potential drivers several options. Get a Chinese person—perhaps a receptionist at your guest house—to draft a letter stating where you would like to go and what you would like to do at your destination—just so you don't end up somewhere you never intended to visit.

Women, as always, should be more careful, and avoid traveling alone if possible. You may or may not be asked to pay for the ride, depending on your location, so it would be good to ask this first and agree on a price before heading off.

Where are you heading?	**Nǐ yào qù nǎr?** 你要去哪儿?
Can you give me a lift?	**Wǒ kěyǐ dā nǐde chē qù ma?** 我可以搭你的车去吗?
Can my friend come too?	**Wǒde péngyou yě néng lái ma?** 我的朋友也能来吗?
I'd like to go to...	**Wǒ xiǎng qù...** 我想去…
Is that on the way to...?	**Zhè shìbushì qù...de lù?** 这是不是去…的路?
Could you drop me off at...?	**Nǐ kěyǐ zài...ràng wǒ xiàchē ma?** 你可以在…让我下车吗?
Could you drop me off here?	**Nǐ kěyǐ zài zhèlǐ ràng wǒ xiàchē ma?** 你可以在这里让我下车吗?
Could you drop me off at the entrance to the highway?	**Nǐ kěyǐ zài gōnglù de jìnkǒu ràng wǒ xiàchē ma?** 你可以在公路的进口让我下车吗?
Could you drop me off at the next intersection highway?	**Nǐ kěyǐ zài xià yí ge shízìlùkǒu ràng wǒ xiàchē ma?** 你可以在下一个十字路口让我下车吗?
Could you stop here, please?	**Nǐ kěyǐ zài zhèlǐ tíngchē ma?** 你可以在这里停车吗?
I'd like to get out here.	**Wǒ xiǎng zài zhèlǐ xiàchē.** 我想在这里下车。
Thanks for the lift.	**Fēicháng gǎnxiè gěi wǒ dāchē.** 非常感谢给我搭车。

6. Arrival and Departure

6.1   General

In China, most people get around by bus (**gōnggòngqìchē** 公共汽车), subway (**dìtiě** 地铁) or taxi (**chūzūchē** 出租车). Although services are frequent, bus stops are often quite a distance apart so many people will be waiting to get on at each stop. It can be quite amazing to see the sheer number of people packed into a bus. Make sure you have change before getting on and be sure to give them the exact amount if possible—they don't give change. In the larger cities, you should be able to get a transportation smart card that will make paying more convenient.

In larger cities, some routes are now serviced by more luxurious air-conditioned buses, which are more comfortable but cost twice as much as the ordinary buses.

Another option is to take taxis or Didi Chuxing, a ridesharing service with an English version of the application for users in Beijing, Shanghai and Guangzhou. The latter means of transport is increasingly preferred by ordinary commuters as they are less expensive than taxis. There are two types of taxis: the less expensive three-seater, and the larger, more comfortable and more expensive five-seater. Payment should be done mostly in cash, but there are some taxis which can also accept your credit cards. It's best to ask once you flag down the taxi. Most major cities also have subways (**dìtiě 地铁**). Tickets are purchased at the stations.

Since 2007 the introduction of high-speed rail in China (**Zhōngguó gāosù tiělù 中国高速铁路**) has enabled commuters to travel speedily across provinces at an average speed of 200 km/h. The Shanghai Maglev train, for example, is able to go beyond 380 km/h but averages 250 km/h because of track constraints. Using such high-speed trains enables the commuter to significantly reduce traveling time.

Inter-city travel is mostly done by train and plane although boats are used to transport passengers along many inland waterways in China. Long-distance travel is mostly done on trains, although domestic air travel has become popular among middle-income earners as airfares are now affordable.

6.2 Immigration and customs

In China, always carry a valid passport with you. Strictly speaking, visitors planning to stay at the same address for more than a week need permission from the Police Department. This is necessary if you intend to study, work or live in China. To drive a car or motorbike, you need an international driving licence.

Foreign currency: you need to declare amounts of foreign currency about US$5,000 or the equivalent, or RMB 20,000, brought into China.

Alcohol: 1.5 liters of spirits or liquor, 1.5 liters of wine
Tobacco: 400 cigarettes, 100 cigars, or 500g tobacco

You must be aged 17 to import alcohol and tobacco and 15 to import coffee and tea. The above restrictions apply to alcohol and tobacco purchased in duty-free shops on arrival.

请填一下入境卡。 **Qǐng tián yíxià rùjìng kǎ.**	Please fill in the arrival card.
请出示你的护照。 **Qǐng chūshì nǐde hùzhào.**	Your passport, please.

请给我看看你的签证。
Qǐng gěi wǒ kànkàn nǐde qiānzhèng.

Your visa, please.

你去哪个城市？
Nǐ qù nǎge chéngshì?

Which city are you going to?

你(们)要在这里住多少天？
Nǐ (men) yào zài zhèlǐ zhù duōshao tiān?

How long are you planning to stay?

你(们)有没有什么要申报？
Nǐ (men) yǒu méiyǒu shénme yào shēnbào?

Do you have anything to declare?

请打开这个箱子。
Qǐng dǎkāi zhè ge xiāngzi.

Open this suitcase, please.

My children are entered on this passport.

Wǒ háizi de míngzi zài wǒde hùzhào shàng. 我孩子的名字在我的护照上。

I'm traveling through.

Wǒ zhǐ shì jīngguò zhèr. 我只是经过这儿。

I'm going on vacation to...

Wǒ yào dào...dùjià 我要到⋯度假

I'm on a business trip.

Wǒ shì lái chūchāi de. 我是来出差的。

I don't know how long I'll be staying.

Wǒ hái bù zhīdao yào zài zhèlǐ zhù duō jiǔ. 我还不知道要在这里住多久。

I'll be staying here for just a weekend.

Wǒ zài zhèlǐ zhǐ zhù yí ge zhōumò. 我在这里只住一个周末。

I'll be staying here for a few days.

Wǒ zài zhèlǐ zhù jǐ tiān. 我在这里住几天。

I'll be staying here for a week.

Wǒ zài zhèlǐ zhù yí ge xīngqí. 我在这里住一个星期。

I'll be staying here for two weeks.

Wǒ zài zhèlǐ zhù liǎng ge xīngqí. 我在这里住两个星期。

I've got nothing to declare.

Wǒ méiyǒu shénme yào shēnbào de. 我没有什么要申报的。

I have a carton of cigarettes.	**Wǒ yǒu yì hé xiāngyān.** 我有一盒香烟。
I have a bottle of whisky.	**Wǒ yǒu yì píng wēishìjì.** 我有一瓶威士忌。
I have some souvenirs.	**Wǒ yǒu yìxiē jìniànpǐn.** 我有一些纪念品。
These are personal items.	**Zhèxiē dōu shì wǒ zìjǐ yòng de dōngxi.** 这些都是我自己用的东西。
These are not new.	**Zhèxiē dōu bú shì xīn de.** 这些都不是新的。
Here's the receipt.	**Zhè shì shōujù.** 这是收据。
This is for private use.	**Zhè shì wǒ sīrén yòng de.** 这是我私人用的。
How much import duty do I have to pay?	**Wǒ yào jiāo duōshao shuì?** 我要交多少税？
May I go now?	**Wǒ kěyǐ zǒu le ma?** 我可以走了吗？
Where do I pick up my luggage?	**Dào nǎli qǔ xíngli?** 到哪里取行李？

6.3 Luggage

Could you take this luggage to...?	**Qǐng bāng wǒ bǎ zhè jiàn xíngli ná dào...** 请帮我把这件行李拿到…
How much do I owe you?	**Wǒ yào fù nǐ duōshao xiǎofèi?** 我要付你多少小费？
Where can I find a trolley?	**Wǒ zài nǎli néng zhǎodào xiǎo tuīchē?** 我在哪里能找到小推车？
Could you store this luggage for me?	**Qǐng gěi wǒ cúnxià zhè jiàn xíngli.** 请给我存下这件行李。
Where are the luggage lockers?	**Xíngli guìzi zài nǎli?** 行李柜子在哪里？

I can't get the locker open.	**Wǒ dǎbukāi zhè ge guìzi.** 我打不开这个柜子。
How much is it per item per day?	**Cún yí jiàn xíngli yì tiān duōshao qián?** 存一件行李一天多少钱？
This is not my bag.	**Zhè bú shì wǒde lǚxíngbāo.** 这不是我的旅行包。
This is not my suitcase.	**Zhè bú shì wǒde xiāngzi.** 这不是我的箱子。
My suitcase is damaged.	**Wǒde xiāngzi bèi záhuàile.** 我的箱子被砸坏了。
There's one item missing.	**Wǒ diūshīle yí jiàn xíngli.** 我丢失了一件行李。
There's one bag missing.	**Wǒ diūshīle yí ge lǚxíngbāo.** 我丢失了一个旅行包。
There's one suitcase missing.	**Wǒ diūshīle yí ge xiāngzi.** 我丢失了一个箱子。
My luggage has not arrived.	**Wǒ de xíngli hǎi méi dàodá.** 我的行李还没到达。
When do you think my luggage will arrive?	**Nǐ rènwéi wǒ de xínglǐ shénme shíhou huì dàodá?** 你认为我的行李什么时候会到达？
Can I get any compensation during this time as my belongings are all in the luggage?	**Yīnwèi wǒ de wùpǐn dōu zài xínglǐxiāng lǐ, zài zhèduàn shíjiān lǐ wǒ kěyǐ dédào rènhé péicháng ma?** 因为我的物品都在行李箱里，在这段时间里我可以得到任何赔偿吗？

Tickets

Where can I buy a ticket?	**Wǒ shàng nǎr kěyǐ mǎi piào?** 我上哪儿可以买票？

Where can I reserve a seat?	**Wǒ shàng nǎr kěyǐ yùdìng wèizi?** 我上哪儿预订位子？
Where can I reserve a flight?	**Wǒ shàng nǎr kěyǐ yùdìng jīpiào?** 我上哪儿预订机票？
Could I have a ticket to Beijing, please?	**Wǒ néng bu néng mǎi yì zhāng qù Běijīng de piào?** 我能不能买一张去北京的票？
A one-way ticket to Beijing please.	**Qǐng gěi wǒ yì zhāng qù Běijīng de dānchéngpiào.** 请给我一张去北京的单程票。
A return ticket to Beijing, please.	**Qǐng gěi wǒ yì zhāng qù Běijīng de láihuípiào.** 请给我一张去北京的来回票。
I'd like to reserve a hard berth.	**Wǒ xiǎng yùdìng yì zhāng yìngwò.** 我想预订一张硬卧。
I'd like to reserve a soft berth.	**Wǒ xiǎng yùdìng yì zhāng ruǎnwò.** 我想预订一张软卧。
I'd like to reserve a top berth in the hard berth car.	**Wǒ xiǎng yùdìng yìngwò chēxiāng de shàngpù.** 我想预订硬卧车厢的上铺。
I'd like to reserve a middle berth in the hard berth car.	**Wǒ xiǎng yùdìng yìngwò chēxiāng de zhōngpù.** 我想预订硬卧车厢的中铺。
I'd like to reserve a bottom berth in the hard berth car.	**Wǒ xiǎng yùdìng yìngwò chēxiāng de xiàpù.** 我想预订硬卧车厢的下铺。
I'd like to reserve a top berth in the soft berth car.	**Wǒ xiǎng yùdìng ruǎnwò chēxiāng de shàngpù.** 我想预订软卧车厢的上铺。
I'd like to reserve a bottom berth in the soft berth car.	**Wǒ xiǎng yùdìng ruǎnwò chēxiāng de xiàpù.** 我想预订软卧车厢的下铺。

6.5 Information

Where can I find a schedule?	**Nǎli yǒu shíkèbiǎo?** 哪里有时刻表？
Where's the information desk?	**Fúwùtái zài nǎli?** 服务台在哪里？
Do you have a city map with the bus routes on it?	**Yǒu méiyǒu shìqū qìchē de lùxiàntú?** 有没有市区汽车的路线图？
Do you have a city map with the subway routes on it?	**Yǒu méiyǒu shìqū dìtiě de lùxiàntú?** 有没有市区地铁的路线图？
Do you have a schedule?	**Yǒu méiyǒu shíkèbiǎo?** 有没有时刻表？
Will I get my deposit back?	**Néng bu néng náhuí yājīn?** 能不能拿回押金？
I'd like to confirm my reservation for my trip to Shanghai.	**Wǒ xiǎng quèrèn wǒ yùdìng qù Shànghǎi de lǚchéng.** 我想确认我预订去上海的旅程。
I'd like to cancel my reservation for my trip to Shanghai.	**Wǒ xiǎng qǔxiāo wǒ yùdìng qù Shànghǎi de lǚchéng.** 我想取消我预订去上海的旅程。
I'd like to change my reservation for my trip to Shanghai.	**Wǒ xiǎng gǎibiàn wǒ yùdìng qù Shànghǎi de lǚchéng.** 我想改变我预订去上海的旅程。
I'd like to go to Shanghai.	**Wǒ xiǎng qù Shànghǎi.** 我想去上海。
What is the quickest way to get there?	**Qù nàbiān zuìkuài de lùchéng shì nǎ yì tiáo?** 去那边最快的路程是哪一条？
How much is a one-way ticket to Shanghai?	**Qù Shànghǎi de dānchéngpiào shì duōshao qián?** 去上海的单程票是多少钱？

| How much is a return ticket to Shanghai? | **Qù Shànghǎi de láihuípiào shì duōshao qián?** 去上海的来回票是多少钱？ |
| How much is a return ticket to Shanghai? | |

| Do I have to pay extra? | **Yào duō fùqián ma?** 要多付钱吗？ |

| How much luggage am I allowed? | **Kěyǐ xiédài duōshao xíngli?** 可以携带多少行李？ |

| Do I have to change buses? | **Yào zhuǎn qìchē ma?** 要转汽车吗？ |

| Do I have to change trains? | **Yào zhuǎn huǒchē ma?** 要转火车吗？ |

| Do I have to change flights? | **Yào zhuǎn fēijī ma?** 要转飞机吗？ |

| Where do I change buses? | **Zài nǎli zhuǎn qìchē?** 在哪里转汽车？ |

| Where do I change trains? | **Zài nǎli zhuǎn huǒchē?** 在哪里转火车？ |

| Where do I change flights? | **Zài nǎli zhuǎn fēijī?** 在哪里转飞机？ |

| Will there be any stopovers? | **Zhōngtú yào tíngliú ma?** 中途要停留吗？ |

| Does the boat stop at any other ports on the way? | **Kèchuán tú zhōng yào tíng qítā mǎtóu ma?** 客船途中要停其他码头吗？ |

| Does the train stop at...? | **Huǒchē zài...tíng ma?** 火车在…停吗？ |

| Does the bus stop at...? | **Qìchē zài...tíng ma?** 汽车在…停吗？ |

| Where do I get off? | **Zài nǎli xià (chē/chuán)?** 在哪里下〔车／船〕？ |

| Is there a connection to...? | **Qù...yǒu liányùn ma?** 去…有连运吗？ |

| How long do I have to wait? | **Yào děng duō jiǔ?** 要等多久？ |

| When does the bus leave? | **Zhè bān qìchē shénme shíhou kāichē?** 这班汽车什么时候开车？ |

| When does the train leave? | **Zhè bān lièchē shénme shíhou kāichē?** 这班列车什么时候开车？ |

| When does the boat leave? | **Zhè bān kèchuán shénme shíhou kāichuán?** 这班客船什么时候开船？ |

When does the plane leave?	**Zhè bān fēijī shénme shíhou qǐfēi?** 这班飞机什么时候起飞?
What time does the first (bus/train) leave?	**Tóubānchē jǐ diǎn kāi?** 头班车几点开?
What time does the last (bus/train) leave?	**Mòbānchē jǐ diǎn kāi?** 末班车几点开?
What time does the first boat leave?	**Tóubānchuán jǐ diǎn kāi?** 头班船几点开?
What time does the last plane leave?	**Mòbānjī jǐ diǎn qǐfēi?** 末班机几点起飞?
What time does the next bus leave?	**Xià yì bān qìchē jǐ diǎn kāi?** 下一班汽车几点开?
What time does the next train leave?	**Xià yì bān lièchē jǐ diǎn kāi?** 下一班列车几点开?
What time does the next boat leave?	**Xià yì bān kèchuán jǐ diǎn kāi?** 下一班客船几点开?
What time does the next plane leave?	**Xià yì bān fēijī jǐ diǎn qǐfēi?** 下一班飞机几点起飞?
How long does...take?	**...xūyào duō cháng shíjiān?** ⋯需要多长时间?
What time does...arrive in...?	**...shénme shíhou dào...?** ⋯什么时候到⋯?
Where does the bus/ train to...leave from?	**Qù...de qìchē/lièchē cóng nǎr líkāi?** 去⋯的汽车／列车从哪儿离开?
Where does the boat to...leave from?	**Qù...de kèchuán cóng nǎr líkāi?** 去⋯的客船从哪儿离开?
Where does the plane to...leave from?	**Qù...de fēijī cóng nǎr líkāi?** 去⋯的飞机从哪儿离开?
Is this the train/bus to...?	**Zhè tàng lièchē/qìché qù...ma?** 这趟列车／汽车去⋯吗?

6.6 Airports

China's international airports are located in large cities and provide high quality transportation. As in other international airport, make sure you have your passport and visa ready before you reach immigration. And make sure you complete your arrival forms. Chinese customs are usually very helpful and friendly, but do not become angry or aggressive with them. This will only cause you a lot of trouble. Do ask for assistance if you have any doubts. Make sure you complete the declaration form before you enter customs because there might be some particular items that need to be declared.

check in
bànlǐ dēngjī
办理登机

check-in counter
dēngjī guìtái
登机柜台

overweight
chāozhòng
超重

(weighing) scale
bàngchèng
磅秤

passenger
lǚkè
旅客

check-in luggage/bags
tuōyùn xínglǐ
托运行李

customs-declaration form
hǎiguān shēnqǐngdān
海关申请单

ticket
jīpiào
机票

passport
hùzhào
护照

visa
qiānzhèng
签证

form
biǎogé
表格

boarding gate
dēngjīmén
登机门

immigration/arrival
rùjìng
入境

airport security
jīchǎng ānjiǎn
机场安检

metal detector
jīnshǔ tàncè mén
金属探测门

terminal
hángzhàn
航站

shuttle bus
jiēbóchē
接驳车

departure
chūjìng
出境

aisle
zǒudào
走道

economy class
jīngjìcāng
经济舱

first class
tóuděngcāng
头等舱

window
kàochuāng
靠窗

seat belt
ānquándài
安全带

boarding pass	duty-free store	seat
dēngjīpái	**miǎnshuìdiàn**	**zuòwèi**
登机牌	免税店	座位

I would like to check in now.
Wǒ yào bànlǐ dēngjī.
我要办理登机。

Where is the check-in counter?
Qǐngwèn, dēngjī guìtái zài nǎr?
请问，登机柜台在哪？

Where is the duty-free store?
Qǐngwèn, miǎnshuì shāngdiàn zài nǎr?
请问，免税商店在哪？

May I see your ticket and passport?
Wǒ kéyǐ kàn yíxià nínde jīpiào hé hùzhào ma?
我可以看一下您的机票和护照吗？

How many bags are you checking in?
Nǐde tuōyùn xínglǐ yǒu jǐjiàn?
你的托运行李有几件？

I want a window and an aisle seat.
Wǒ yào yíge kàochuāng hé yíge kào zǒudào de zuòwèi.
我要一个靠窗和一个靠走道的座位。

Please put all metal objects in this tray and then walk through the metal detector.
Qǐng bǎ jīnshǔ wùpǐn fàng zài pánzi shàng, jiēzhe zǒuguò jīnshǔ tàncè mén.
请把金属物品放在盘子上，接着走过金属探测门。

All passengers on flight DL 148 should proceed to gate eight for boarding.
DL 148 de lǚkè qǐng dào bāhào dēngjīmén dēngjī.
DL 148的旅客请到八号登机门登机。

Please fasten your seat belt.
Qǐng jìshàng ānquándài.
请系上安全带。

Please fill in the customs-declaration form.
Qǐng tiánxiě hǎiguān shēnqǐngbiǎo.
请填写海关申请表。

Are there any duty-free stores at Terminal One?
Qǐngwèn, dìyī hángzhàn yǒu miǎnshuì shāngdiàn ma?
请问，第一航站有免税商店吗？

Your attention please, the next station is Qianmen.

Gèwèi chéngkè, nín hǎo! Lièchē yùnxíng qiánfāng shì Qiánménzhàn.
各位乘客，您好! 列车运行前方是
前门站。

Passengers getting off at Qianmen, please get ready.

Zài Qiánménzhàn xiàchē de chéngkè, qǐng nín tíqián zuòhǎo zhǔnbèi.
在前门站下车的乘客，请您提前作好
准备。

Qianmen station is a crowded station, please get ready beforehand and alight in an orderly manner.

Qiánménzhàn shàngxiàchē de chéngkè bǐjiào duō, qǐng nín tíqián zuòhǎo zhǔnbèi, àn shùnxù xiàchē.
前门站上下车的乘客比较多，请您提
前作好准备，按顺序下车。

Passengers changing to Gongzhufen Number 1 Line trains please get off at Fuxingmen.

Qiánwǎng Gōngzhǔfén fāngxiàng de chéngkè, qǐng zài Fùxīngmén xiàchē, huànchéng Yīhàoxiàn lièchē.
前往公主坟方向的乘客，请在复兴门
下车，换乘一号线列车。

The train to Fuxingmen is now arriving at platform 3.

Kāiwǎng Fùxīngmén de lièchē, xiànzài dàodá sān hào zhàntái.
开往复兴门的列车，现在到达三号站台。

The train from Qianmen is now arriving at platform 5.

Cóng Qiánménzhàn kāichū de lièchē, xiànzài dàodá wǔ hào zhàntái.
从前门站开出的列车，现在到达五号
站台。

The train to Fuxingmen will leave from platform 3.

Kāiwǎng Fùxīngmén de lièchē, jiāng zài sān hào zhàntái lízhàn.
开往复兴门的列车，将在三号站台离站。

Today the 9 a.m. train to Fuxingmen will leave from platform 3.

Jīntiān jiǔ diǎn kāiwǎng Fùxīngmén de lièchē, jiāng zài sān hào zhàntái lízhàn.
今天九点开往复兴门的列车，将在三号
站台离站。

The next station is Qianmen.	**Lièchē yùnxíng qiánfāng shì Qiánménzhàn.** 列车运行前方是前门站。
Where does this train go to?	**Zhè cì lièchē kāiwǎng nǎli?** 这次列车开往哪里？
Does this train stop at Wangfujing?	**Zhè cì lièchē zài Wángfǔjǐng tíng ma?** 这次列车在王府井停吗？
Could you tell me where I have to get off for Wangfujing?	**Qǐngwèn, wǒ dào Wángfǔjǐng gāi zài nǎr xiàchē?** 请问，我到王府井该在哪儿下车？
Could you let me know when we get to Wangfujing?	**Dào Wángfǔjǐng de shíhou, qǐng gàosu wǒ yì shēng.** 到王府井的时候，请告诉我一声。
Could you stop at the next stop, please?	**Máfan nín, xià ge zhàn wǒ děi xiàchē.** 麻烦您，下个站我得下车。
Where are we?	**Wǒmen xiànzài zài nǎli?** 我们现在在哪里？
Can I get off the train for a while?	**Kěyǐ xiàchē kànkan ma?** 可以下车看看吗？
Do I get off here?	**Wǒ zài zhèlǐ xiàchē ma?** 我在这里下车吗？
Have we already passed Wangfujing?	**Guòle Wángfǔjǐng méiyǒu?** 过了王府井没有？
How long does the train stop here?	**Lièchē zài zhèlǐ tíng duō cháng shíjiān?** 列车在这里停多长时间？
Will we arrive on time?	**Wǒmen huì zhǔnshí dàodá ma?** 我们会准时到达吗？
Is this seat taken?	**Zhè ge wèizi yǒu rén zuò ma?** 这个位子有人坐吗？
Excuse me, this is my seat.	**Duìbuqǐ, zhè shì wǒde wèizi.** 对不起，这是我的位子。

6.8 Long-distance trains

Train travel in China is a good way to see the country. Long-distance trains are generally quite comfortable if you travel on the "soft class" (**ruǎnxí wòpù** 软席卧铺). The "soft class" car has a number of cabins each with four berths, a small table, and a sliding door. The "hard class" (**yìngxí wòpù** 硬席卧铺) has six berths opening to a common walkway. There are toilets at the end of each car. Foreigners and Chinese business people generally take the more expensive but more comfortable "soft class". All train travelers are provided with free boiling water and they can order inexpensive meals.

Ticket types

What types of tickets would you like to buy?	**Nín xiǎng mǎi nǎ zhǒng piào?** 您想买哪种票？
Hard seat or soft seat?	**Yìngzuò háishi ruǎnzuò?** 硬座还是软座？
Hard berth or soft berth?	**Yìngwò háishi ruǎnwò?** 硬卧还是软卧？
There are three types of hard berths: top, middle or bottom.	**Yìngwò yǒu sān zhǒng: shàngpù, zhōngpù hé xiàpù.** 硬卧有三种：上铺，中铺和下铺。
Which types of hard berths do you want: top, middle or bottom?	**Nǐ xiǎng yào shénme yìngwò: shàngpù, zhōngpù háishi xiàpù?** 你想要什么硬卧：上铺，中铺还是下铺？
There are two types of soft berths: top or bottom.	**Ruǎnwò yǒu liǎng zhǒng: shàngpù hé xiàpù.** 软卧有两种：上铺和下铺。
Which types of soft berths do you want: top or bottom?	**Nǐ xiǎng yào shénme ruǎnwò: shàngpù háishi xiàpù?** 你想要什么软卧：上铺还是下铺？

Traveling by train

destination	**mùdìdì** 目的地
Which city are you traveling to?	**Nǐ(men) qù nǎ ge chéngshì?** 你(们)去哪个城市?
When are you leaving?	**Nǐ(men) shénme shíhou qù?** 你(们)什么时候去?
Your train leaves at 9 a.m.	**Nǐ(men) de lièchē jiǔ diǎn kāi.** 你(们)的列车九点开。
You have to change trains.	**Nǐ(men) yào zhuǎnchē.** 你(们)要转车。
You have to get off at Qianmen.	**Nǐ(men) yào zài Qiánménzhàn xiàchē.** 你(们)要在前门站下车。
Tickets, please.	**Qǐng chūshì piào.** 请出示票。
Your reservation, please.	**Qǐng bǎ nǐ yùdìng de piào gěi wǒ kànkan.** 请把你预订的票给我看看。
Your passport, please.	**Qǐng bǎ nǐde hùzhào gěi wǒ kànkan.** 请把你的护照给我看看。
You're in the wrong seat.	**Nǐ(men) zuòcuò wèizile.** 你(们)坐错位子了。
You have made a mistake.	**Nǐ(men) nòngcuòle.** 你(们)弄错了。
This seat is reserved.	**Zhè ge zuòr yǒu rén yùdìngle.** 这个座儿有人预订了。
You'll have to pay extra.	**Nǐ(men) yào bǔpiào.** 你(们)要补票。
The train has been delayed by 10 minutes.	**Lièchē wǎndiǎn shí fēnzhōng.** 列车晚点十分钟。

6.9 Buses

Excuse me, which bus should I take to get to Wangfujing?	**Qǐngwèn, qù Wángfǔjǐng gāi zuò jǐlù gōnggòngqìchē?** 请问,去王府井该坐几路公共汽车?

You can catch the 103 trolley bus.	**Kěyǐ zuò yāolíngsān lù wúguǐdiànchē.** 可以坐一零三路无轨电车。
Excuse me, where should I change (to another) bus to get to the Australian embassy?	**Qǐngwèn, qù Àozhōu dàshǐguǎn zài shénme dìfang huànchē?** 请问，去澳洲大使馆在什么地方换车？
There's no need to change (to another) bus, take bus 318 till the terminal.	**Búyào zhuǎnchē, nín zuò sānyāobā lù yīzhí dào zhōngdiǎn.** 不要转车，您坐三一八路一直到终点。
We've arrived at Sun Yat-Sen Park. Passengers please get off now.	**Zhōngshān gōngyuán dàole, qǐng xiàchē.** 中山公园到了，请下车。
Next stop is Xidan, please get ready to get off.	**Xià yí zhàn Xīdān, qǐng nín zhǔnbèi xiàchē.** 下一站西单，请您准备下车。
Please let the passengers get off first to ensure safety.	**Qǐng nín xiānxià hòushàng, zhùyì ānquán.** 请您先下后上，注意安全。
The bus is moving, please hold onto the hand grips.	**Chē yào qǐdòng, qǐng lāhǎo fúshǒu.** 车要起动，请拉好扶手。
What's the frequency of service for bus 101?	**Yāolíngyāo lù qìchē de chēcì duō bu duō?** 一零一路汽车的车次多不多？
The frequency of service for bus 101 is every three minutes.	**Yāolíngyāo lù qìchē de chēcì hěnduō, měi sān fēnzhōng yí tàng.** 一零一路汽车的车次很多，每三分钟一趟。
What's the earliest bus service for bus 107?	**Yāolíngqī lù qìchē de tóubānchē shì shénme shíjiān?** 一零七路汽车的头班车是什么时间？
The earliest bus service for bus 107 is 5:45 a.m.	**Yāolíngqī lù qìchē de tóubānchē shì zǎoshang wǔdiǎn sìshíwǔ fēn.** 一零七路汽车的头班车是早上五点四十五分。

| What's the last bus service for bus 107? | **Yāolíngqī lù qìchē de mòbānchē shì shénme shíjiān?**
一零七路汽车的末班车是什么时间? |
| The last bus service for bus 107 is 11:30 p.m. | **Yāolíngqī lù qìchē de mòbānchē shì wǎnshang shíyīdiǎnbàn.**
一零七路汽车的末班车是晚上十一点半。 |

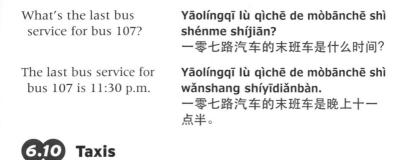 **6.10** Taxis

Taxis provide a reasonably priced and efficient means of getting about most of China's major cities. Taxis at hotels are generally more spacious and thus more expensive than those you hail on the street. You may want to ask your driver (**sījī** 司机) to wait for you while you are on sightseeing trips or finishing your business—the cost for waiting for you is not expensive. It's an excellent idea to ask someone to write down your destination in Chinese before you take a taxi.

You can also rent your own taxi with its driver for a day or two. This is a good way to see a lot of the sights at your own pace. Price is negotiable with the driver. If you can split the cost with your companions, the price is generally reasonable.

| for hire
chūzū
出租 | occupied
yǒu'rén
有人 | taxi stand
chūzū qìchēzhàn
出租汽车站 |

Taxi!	**Chūzūchē!** 出租车!
Could you get me a taxi please?	**Qǐng bāng wǒ jiào yí liàng chūzūchē.** 请帮我叫一辆出租车。
Where can I find a taxi around here?	**Nǎli yǒu chūzūchē?** 哪里有出租车?
Could you take me to this address, please?	**Qǐng dài wǒ dào zhè ge dìzhǐ.** 请带我到这个地址。
Could you take me to the X hotel, please?	**Qǐng dài wǒ dào X bīn'guǎn/lǚguǎn.** 请带我到X宾馆／旅馆。

Could you take me to the town/city center, please? **Qǐng dài wǒ dào chénglǐ.** 请带我到城里。

Could you take me to the Qianmen station, please? **Qǐng dài wǒ dào Qiánménzhàn.** 请带我到前门站。

Could you take me to the airport, please? **Qǐng dài wǒ dào jīchǎng.** 请带我到机场。

How much is the trip to the airport? **Qù jīchǎng duōshao qiǎn?** 去机场多少钱？

How far is it to the airport? **Zhèlǐ lí jīchǎng yǒu duō yuǎn?** 这里离机场有多远？

Could you turn on the meter, please (driver)? **Sījī, qǐng nǐ dǎbiǎo.** 司机，请你打表。

I'm in a hurry. **Wǒ zài gǎn shíjiān.** 我在赶时间。

Could you speed up a little? **Néng kāi de kuài yìdiǎn ma?** 能开得快一点吗？

Could you slow down a little? **Néng kāi de màn yìdiǎn ma?** 能开得慢一点吗？

Could you take a different route? **Néng zǒu lìng yì tiáo lù ma?** 能走另一条路吗？

I'd like to get out here, please. **Wǒ zài zhèlǐ xiàchē.** 我在这里下车。

How much does it cost to hire a driver per day? **Zū sījī yì tiān yào duōshao qián?** 租司机一天 要多少钱？

How much does it cost to hire a driver for two days? **Zū sījī liǎng tiān yào duōshao qián?** 租司机两天要多少钱？

How many kilometers per day do I get for the basic fee? **Měitiān de jīběn fèiyòng néng bàoxiāo duōshao gōnglǐ?** 每天的基本费用能报销多少公里？

Does the price include gas? **Jiàqián bàokuò qìyóu fèi ma?** 价钱包括汽油费吗？

Can the driver speak English?	**Sījī huì shuō Yīngyǔ ma?** 司机会说英语吗?
Will the driver stay with me all day?	**Sījī zhěngtiān dōu péizhe wǒ ma?** 司机整天都陪着我吗?
Shall I take care of the driver's meals?	**Wǒ yào fùzé sījī de fànqián ma?** 我要负责司机的饭钱吗?
Do I settle the cost with the driver at the end of the day?	**Wǒ zài yì tiān jié shù shí gēn sījī jiézhàng ma?** 我在一天结束时跟司机结账吗?
Go.	**Zǒu ba.** 走吧。
You have to go right here.	**Yào cóng zhèlǐ...qù** 要从这里…去
Go straight ahead.	**Yìzhí zǒu.** 一直走。
Turn left.	**Zhuǎn zuǒ.** 转左。
Turn right.	**Zhuǎn yòu.** 转右。
This is it.	**Zhèlǐ jiù shì.** 这里就是。
We're here.	**Dàole.** 到了。
Could you wait a while for me, please?	**Nǐ néng děng wǒ yíhuìr ma?** 你能等我一会儿吗?
How much is it?	**Duōshao qián?** 多少钱?

7. A Place to Stay

7.1 General
7.2 Hotels/hostels/budget accommodations
7.3 Requests
7.4 Complaints
7.5 Departure

 **General**

In China, hotels for foreigners range from the basic two-star twin share accommodation with own bathroom (**lǚguǎn** 旅馆) in small towns and outlying areas to five-star accommodations (**bīn'guǎn/jiǔdiàn** 宾馆／酒店) with swimming pools, sauna, restaurants etc., in capital cities. Hotels around railway stations generally cater mainly for Chinese travelers with basic accommodation (**zhāodàisuǒ** 招待所). Increasingly there are youth hostels for foreign backpackers in major cities such as Beijing. You can also book your accommodation online prior to your trip from Booking.com, Agoda.com or Ctrip.com. Be sure to bring your booking confirmation along.

Do you have any rooms available?	**Nǐmen yǒu méiyǒu kōng fáng?** 你们有没有空房？
I'm looking for a cheap hotel.	**Wǒ yào zhǎo yì jiā piányi de lǚguǎn.** 我要找一家便宜的旅馆。
I'm looking for a nearby hotel.	**Wǒ yào zhǎo yì jiā línjìn de lǚguǎn.** 我要找一家邻近的旅馆。
Do you give discounts for students?	**Nǐmen duì liúxuéshēng yǒu méiyǒu yōuhuì?** 你们对留学生有没有优惠？
I'm not sure how long I'm staying.	**Wǒ hái bù zhīdao yào zhù duō jiǔ.** 我还不知道要住多久。
Do you have air-conditioning in the room?	**Fángjiān lǐ yǒu méiyǒu kōngtiáo?** 房间里有没有空调？

Do you have heating in the room?	**Fángjiān lǐ yǒu méiyǒu nuǎnqì?** 房间里有没有暖气?
Do you have hot water all day?	**Nǐmen zhěng tiān dōu yǒu rèshuǐ ma?** 你们整天都有热水吗?
When is the heating turned on?	**Shénme shíhou cái kāi nuǎnqì?** 什么时候才开暖气?
Do you have room service?	**Nǐmen yǒu méiyǒu kèfáng fúwù?** 你们有没有客房服务?
Where's the emergency exit?	**Jǐnjí chūkǒu zài nǎr?** 紧急出口在哪儿?
Where's the fire escape?	**Ánquán chūkǒu zài nǎr?** 安全出口在哪儿?
Can I have two keys, please?	**Qǐng gěi wǒ liǎng bǎ yàoshi.** 请给我两把钥匙。
The key to room 602, please.	**Qǐng gěi wǒ liù líng èr hào fángjiān de yàoshi.** 请给我六零二号房间的钥匙。
Could you put this in the safe, please?	**Qǐng bǎ zhège dōngxi fàng zài bǎoxiǎnxiāng lǐ.** 请把这个东西放在保险箱里。
Could you wake me at 7 a.m., tomorrow?	**Míngtiān qǐng zài qīdiǎn jiàoxǐng wǒ.** 明天请在七点叫醒我。
Could I have an extra blanket?	**Kěyǐ zài gěi wǒ yì chuáng tǎnzi ma?** 可以再给我一床毯子吗?
What time does the gatc/door open?	**Dàmén jǐ diǎnzhōng kāi?** 大门几点钟开?
What time does the gate/door close?	**Dàmén jǐ diǎnzhōng guān?** 大门几点钟关?
Could you get me a taxi, please?	**Qǐng gěi wǒ jiào yí liàng chūzūchē, hǎo ma?** 请给我叫一辆出租车, 好吗?
Could you find a babysitter for me?	**Kěyǐ gěi wǒ zhǎo ge línshí bǎomǔ ma?** 可以给我找个临时保姆吗?
Is there any mail for me?	**Yǒu méiyǒu wǒde xìn?** 有没有我的信?

请填这张表格。 Fill out this form, please.
Qǐng tián zhè zhāng biǎogé.

请给我看看你的护照。 Could I see your passport?
Qǐng gěi wǒ kànkan nǐde hùzhào.

你需要交押金。 You need to put a deposit.
Nǐ xūyào jiāo yājīn.

7.2 Hotels/hostels/budget accommodations

Booking

My name is...	**Wǒde míngzi shì...** 我的名字是…
I've reserved a room.	**Wǒ yǐjīng yùdìngle fángjiān.** 我已经预订了房间。
I emailed you last month.	**Wǒ zài shàng ge yuè fā diànzǐ yóujiàn gěi nǐmen.** 我在上个月发电子邮件给你们。
Here's the confirmation.	**Zhè shì quèrèndān.** 这是确认单。
How much is it per night?	**Wǒ zhù de fángjiān duōshao qián yì tiān?** 我住的房间多少钱一天？
How much is it per week?	**Wǒ zhù de fángjiān duōshao qián yì ge xīngqí?** 我住的房间多少钱一个星期？
We'll be staying for two nights.	**Wǒmen dǎsuàn zhù liǎng tiān.** 我们打算住两天。
We'll be staying for two weeks.	**Wǒmen dǎsuàn zhù liǎng ge xīngqí.** 我们打算住两个星期。
I'd like a single room.	**Wǒ yào yì jiān dānrénfáng.** 我要一间单人房。
I'd like a double room.	**Wǒ yào yì jiān shuāngrénfáng.** 我要一间双人房。
per person	**yí ge rén** 一个人
per room	**yì jiān fáng** 一间房

I'd like a room with twin beds.	**Wǒ yào yī jiān yǒu liǎng zhāng chuáng de fángjiān.** 我要一间有两张床的房间。
I'd like a room with a double bed.	**Wǒ yào yī jiān yǒu yì zhāng shuāngrénchuáng de fángjiān.** 我要一间有一张双人床的房间。
I'd like a room with a bath tub.	**Wǒ yào yī jiān yǒu yùpén de fángjiān.** 我要一间有浴盆的房间。
I'd like a room with a shower.	**Wǒ yào yī jiān yǒu línyù de fángjiān.** 我要一间有淋浴的房间。
I'd like a room with a shower.	**Wǒ yào yī jiān yǒu yángtái de fángjiān.** 我要一间有阳台的房间。
I'd like a suite.	**Wǒ yào yì jiān tàofáng.** 我要一间套房
Could we have adjoining rooms?	**Wǒmen néng bu néng zhù gébì?** 我们能不能住隔壁?
We'd like a room facing the front.	**Wǒmen yào yì jiān cháo qiān de fáng.** 我们要一间朝前的房。
We'd like a room at the back.	**Wǒmen yào yì jiān cháo hòu de fáng.** 我们要一间朝后的房。
We'd like a room with a view of the street.	**Wǒmen yào yì jiān miànduì dàjiē de fáng.** 我们要一间面对大街的房。
We'd like a room with a view of the river.	**Wǒmen yào yì jiān miànduì hé de fáng.** 我们要一间面对河的房。
We'd like a room with a view of the sea.	**Wǒmen yào yì jiān miànduì hǎi de fáng.** 我们要一间面对海的房。
We'd like a non-smoking room.	**Wǒmen yào yì jiān fēi xīyān de fáng.** 我们要一间非吸烟的房。
Does that include breakfast?	**Fángjià bāokuò zǎocān ma?** 房价包括早餐吗?
Does that include lunch?	**Fángjià bāokuò wǔcan ma?** 房价包括午餐吗?
Does that include dinner?	**Fángjià bāokuò wǎncān ma?** 房价包括晚餐吗?

Is there air-conditioning in the room?

Fángjiān lǐ yǒu méiyǒu kōngtiáo?
房间里有没有空调？

Is there heating in the room?

Fángjiān lǐ yǒu méiyǒu nuǎnqì?
房间里有没有暖气？

Is there a TV in the room?

Fángjiān lǐ yǒu méiyǒu diànshìjī?
房间里有没有电视机？

Is there a refrigerator in the room?

Fángjiān lǐ yǒu méiyǒu diànbīngxiāng?
房间里有没有电冰箱？

Is there hot water in the room?

Fángjiān lǐ yǒu méiyǒu rèshuǐ?
房间里有没有热水？

Is there an electric kettle in the room?

Fángjiān lǐ yǒu méiyǒu diànshuǐhú?
房间里有没有电水壶？

Is there free Wi-Fi in the room?

Fángjiān lǐ yǒu méiyǒu miánfèide wǔxiàn shàngwǎng?
房间里有没有免费的无线上网？

Hotels

Could I see the room?

Wǒ néng kànkan fángjiān ma?
我能看看房间吗？

We don't like this one.

Wǒmen bù xǐhuan zhè jiān.
我们不喜欢这间。

Do you have another room?

Hái yǒu biéde fángjiān ma?
还有别的房间吗？

Do you have a larger room?

Yǒu dàyìdiǎnde fángjiān ma?
有大一点的房间吗？

Do you have a less expensive room?

Yǒu gèng piányi de fángjiān ma?
有更便宜的房间吗？

We prefer a quiet room.

Wǒmen xǐhuan ānjìng de fángjiān.
我们喜欢安静的房间。

No, they are all occupied.

Méiyǒu le, dōu zhùmǎn le.
没有了，都住满了。

This room is too hot.

Zhè fángjiān tài rè le. 这房间太热了。

This room is too cold.

Zhè fángjiān tài lěng le.
这房间太冷了。

This room is too dark. **Zhè fángjiān tài àn le.** 这房间太暗了。

This room is too small. **Zhè fángjiān tài xiǎo le.**
这房间太小了。

This room is too noisy. **Zhè fángjiān tài cáozá le.**
这房间太嘈杂了。

I'll take this room. **Wǒ jiù yào zhè ge fángjiān.**
我就要这个房间。

Could you put in a cot? **Néng jiā fàng yì zhāng yīng'érchuáng
ma?** 能加放一张婴儿床吗？

What time's breakfast? **Jǐ diǎn chī zǎocān?** 几点吃早餐？

Where's the dining room? **Cāntīng zài nǎlǐ?** 餐厅在哪里？

Can I have breakfast in
my room? **Kěyǐ zài fángjiān lǐ chī zǎocān ma?**
可以在房间里吃早餐吗？

请跟我来。
Qǐng gēn wǒ lái.

This way please.

你的房间在···层／楼，···号房间
**Nǐ de fángjiān zài... céng/lóu,
...hào fángjiān**

Your room is on the...floor,
number...

厕所和淋浴室在同一层。
Cèsuǒ hé línyù shì zài tóngyīcéng.

The toilet and shower are on
the same floor.

厕所和淋浴室在同一房间。
**Cèsuǒ hé línyù shì zài tóngyī
fángjiān.**

The toilet and shower are in
the room.

How much is the room
per night? **Zhè zhǒng fángjiān duōshao qián
yì wǎn?** 这种房间多少钱一晚？

Does this include
breakfast? **Zhè ge fángjià shìfǒu bāokuò zǎocān?**
这个房价是否包括早餐？

Does this include all
three meals? **Zhè ge fángjià shìfǒu bāokuò sāncān?**
这个房价是否包括三餐？

Does this include the
service charge? **Zhè ge fángjià shìfǒu bāokuò fúwùfèi?**
这个房价是否包括服务费？

I need a two-prong plug. **Wǒ xūyào yí ge shuāngxiàn shìpèiqì.**
我需要一个双线适配器。

I need a three-prong plug. **Wǒ xūyào yí ge sānxiàn shìpèiqì.**
我需要一个三线适配器。

I need this kind of plug. **Wǒ xūyào zhè zhǒng chātóu.**
我需要这种插头。

Where's the plug for the razor? **Guāhúdāo de chāzuò zài nǎli?**
刮胡刀的插座在哪里?

What's the voltage? **Zhèlǐ de diànyā shì duōshao fú?**
这里的电压是多少伏?

May I have some hangers? **Néng bu néng gěi wǒ yìxiē yījià?**
能不能给我一些衣架?

May I have some blankets? **Néng bu néng gěi wǒ yìxiē tǎnzi?**
能不能给我一些毯子?

May I have a needle and some thread? **Néng bu néng gěi wǒ yì gēn zhēn hé yìxiē xiàn?**
能不能给我一根针和一些线?

May I have another pillow? **Néng bu néng gěi wǒ duō yí ge zhěntou?**
能不能给我多一个枕头?

May I have some stationery? **Néng bu néng gěi wǒ yìxiē xìnzhǐ?**
能不能给我一些信纸?

May I have some soap? **Néng bu néng gěi wǒ yìxiē féizào?**
能不能给我一些肥皂?

May I have a bottle of shampoo? **Néng bu néng gěi wǒ yì píng xǐfàjì?**
能不能给我一瓶洗发剂?

May I have a bottle of shower gel? **Néng bu néng gěi wǒ yì píng mùyùyè?**
能不能给我一瓶沐浴液?

May I have another bath towel? **Néng bu néng gěi wǒ duō yí ge yùjīn?**
能不能给我多一个浴巾?

May I have a bottle of cold water (to drink)? **Néng bu néng gěi wǒ yì píng liáng kāishuǐ?** 能不能给我一瓶凉开水?

May I have a flask of hot water (to drink)?	**Néng bu néng gěi wǒ yì hǔ rè kāishuǐ?** 能不能给我一壶热开水？
Can you repair this camera?	**Nǐ néng bu néng bāng wǒ dàixiū zhège zhàoxiàngjī?** 你能不能帮我代修这个照相机？
Can you repair this video camera?	**Nǐ néng bu néng bāng wǒ dàixiū zhège shèxiàngjī?** 你能不能帮我代修这个摄相机？
Can you repair this suitcase?	**Nǐ néng bu néng bāng wǒ dàixiū zhège xiāngzi?** 你能不能帮我代修这个箱子？
The room needs to be cleaned.	**Néng bu néng dǎsǎo yíxià wǒ de fángjiān?** 能不能打扫一下我的房间？
Please change the sheets.	**Qǐng huàn yíxià chuángdān.** 请换一下床单。
Please change the towels.	**Qǐng huàn yíxià máojīn.** 请换一下毛巾。
Please send my breakfast to my room.	**Qǐng bǎ zǎocān sòngdào wǒde fángjiān lǐ.** 请把早餐送到我的房间里。
Please send my lunch to my room.	**Qǐng bǎ wǔcān sòngdào wǒde fángjiān lǐ.** 请把午餐送到我的房间里。
Please send my dinner to my room.	**Qǐng bǎ wǎncān sòngdào wǒde fángjiān lǐ.** 请把晚餐送到我的房间里。
I'd like these clothes washed.	**Qǐng bǎ zhèxiē yīfu xǐgānjìng.** 请把这些衣服洗干净。
I'd like these clothes ironed.	**Qǐng bǎ zhèxiē yīfu yùnhǎo.** 请把这些衣服熨好。
I'd like these clothes dry-cleaned.	**Qǐng bǎ zhèxiē yīfu gānxǐ.** 请把这些衣服干洗。
I'm leaving tonight. Can I put my laundry in?	**Wǒ jīntiān wǎnshang zǒu, hái néng xǐ yīfu ma?** 我今天晚上走，还能洗衣服吗？

Is my laundry ready?	**Wǒde yīfu xǐhǎole ma?** 我的衣服洗好了吗？
I need it today.	**Wǒ yào jīntiān qǔ.** 我要今天取。
I need it tonight.	**Wǒ yào jīnwǎn qǔ.** 我要今晚取。
I need it tomorrow.	**Wǒ yào míngtiān qǔ.** 我要明天取。
I want it as soon as possible.	**Wǒ xīwàng néng yuè kuài yuè hǎo.** 我希望能越快越好。
Can you sew on this button?	**Qǐng gěi wǒ féng yí ge kòuzi.** 请给我缝一个扣子。
This isn't mine.	**Zhè bú shì wǒde.** 这不是我的。
There is one piece missing.	**Wǒ shǎole yí jiàn yīfu.** 我少了一件衣服。
I'm leaving soon, but my laundry is not back yet.	**Wǒ yào zǒu le, xǐ de yīfu hái méiyǒu sònglái ne.** 我要走了，洗的衣服还没有送来呢。

 Complaints

We can't sleep because of the noise.	**Shēngyīn tài cáozá le, wǒmen shuìbuzháo.** 声音太嘈杂了，我们睡不着。
Could you turn the radio down, please?	**Qǐng tiáodī yíxià shōuyīnjī.** 请调低一下收音机。
We're out of toilet paper.	**Shǒuzhǐ/wèishēngzhǐ yòngwánle.** 手纸／卫生纸用完了。
There aren't any...	**Méiyǒu... le** 没有…了
There's not enough...	**...Búgòu** …不够
The bed linen's dirty.	**Chuángdān shì zāng de.** 床单是脏的。
The room hasn't been cleaned.	**Fángjiān méiyǒu shōushí.** 房间没有收拾。
The heating isn't working.	**Nuǎnqì yǒu wèntí, búrè.** 暖气有问题，不热。

There's no hot water.   **Méiyǒu rè shuǐ.** 没有热水。

There's no electricity.   **Méiyǒu diàn.** 没有电。

...doesn't work   **...yǒu máobìng** ⋯有毛病

...is broken   **...huài le** ⋯坏了

The toilet is blocked.   **Cèsuǒ dǔsè le.** 厕所堵塞了。

The sink is blocked.   **Shuǐcáo dǔsè le.** 水槽堵塞了。

The tap is dripping.   **Shuǐlóngtóu lòushuǐ le.**
水龙头漏水了。

The bulb is burnt out.   **Déngpào huài le.** 灯泡坏了。

The blind is broken.   **Bǎiyèchuāng lābudòng le.**
百叶窗拉不动了。

Could you have that
   seen to?   **Qǐng nín zhǎo rén xiū yíxià.**
请您找人修一下。

Could I have another
   room?   **Wǒ kěyǐ lìng yào yì jiān fángjiān ma?**
我可以另要一间房间吗？

The bed creaks terribly.   **Chuáng xiǎngde lìhai.** 床响得厉害。

The bed sags.   **Chuáng huì āoxiàqù.** 床会凹下去。

It's too noisy.   **Zhèr tài cháo le.** 这儿太吵了。

This place is full of
   mosquitos.   **Zhèlǐ dàochù dōu shì wénzi.**
这里到处都是蚊子。

This place is full of
   cockroaches.   **Zhèlǐ dàochù dōu shì zhāngláng.**
这里到处都是蟑螂。

7.5   Departure

See also 8.2 Settling the bill

I'm leaving (the hotel)
   tomorrow.   **Wǒ míngtiān líkāi (lǚdiàn).**
我明天离开(旅店)。

Where can I pay my bill,
   please?   **Qǐngwèn, wǒ dào nǎli fù fángfèi?**
请问，我到哪里付房费？

My room number is 602.
Wǒde fánghào shì liù líng èr hào.
我的房号是六零二号。

What time should we
check out?
**Wǒmen yīnggāi jǐdiǎn bàn lídiàn
shǒuxù?** 我们应该几点办离店手续？

I'm leaving early
tomorrow. Please
prepare the bill.
**Wǒ míngtiān hěn zǎo jiù yào zǒu,
qǐng zhǔnbèihǎo zhàngdān.**
我明天很早就要走，请准备好账单。

Could I have my deposit
back, please?
Qǐng huán gěi wǒ yājīn.
请还给我押金。

I must leave at once.
Wǒ bìxū mǎshàng líkāi.
我必须马上离开。

Is this my bill?
Zhè shì wǒde zhàngdān ma?
这是我的账单吗？

Is everything included?
Suǒyǒu fèiyòng dōu bāokuò le ma?
所有费用都包括了吗？

Do you accept credit
cards?
Nǐmen jiēshòu xìnyòngkǎ ma?
你们接受信用卡吗？

I reckon you've made
a mistake in the bill.
**Wǒ rènwéi zhàngdān shàng yǒu yí chù
cuòwù.** 我认为账单上有一处错误。

Could you forward my
mail to this address?
**Qǐng bǎ wǒde yóujiàn jìdào zhè ge
dìzhǐ.** 请把我的邮件寄到这个地址。

Could I leave my luggage
here until I leave?
**Xíngli liú zài zhèlǐ děng wǒ zǒu
yǐqián zài qǔ, kěyǐ ma?**
行李留在这里等我走以前再取，
可以吗？

Thanks for your
hospitality
Gǎnxiè nǐmende rèqíng zhāodài.
感谢你们的热情招待。

We enjoyed it, thank you.
Wǒmen zhùde hěn mǎnyì, xièxie.
我们住得很满意，谢谢。

8. Money Matters

8.1 Banks
8.2 Settling the bill

In general, banks are open Monday to Friday from 9 a.m. to 5 p.m., but it is always possible to exchange money in hotels or other tourist shops. Your passport is usually needed to do so. Travelers' checks can be cashed and bought at major banks, but are usually only accepted by large hotels and tourist shops. You can also withdraw money from the local Bank of China, Merchant Bank and Industrial and Commercial Bank of China ATMs, which can be easily found in the major cities.

 Banks

Where can I change foreign currency?	**Shàng nǎr kěyǐ huàn wàibì?** 上哪儿可以换外币？
Where can I find the Bank of China around here?	**Zhèlǐ nǎli yǒu Zhōngguó Yínháng?** 这里哪里有中国银行？
Can I cash this traveler's check here?	**Kěyǐ zài zhèlǐ duìhuàn lǚxíng zhīpiào ma?** 可以在这里兑换旅行支票吗？
What's today's exchange rate for US dollars to Chinese yuan?	**Jīntiān Měiyuán duìhuàn Rénmínbì de duìhuànlǜ shì duōshao?** 今天美元兑换人民币的兑换率是多少？
What's today's exchange rate for the British pound to Chinese yuan?	**Jīntiān Yīngbàng duìhuàn Rénmínbì de duìhuànlǜ shì duōshao?** 今天英镑兑换人民币的兑换率是多少？
What's today's exchange rate for the Japanese yen to Chinese yuan?	**Jīntiān Rìyuán duìhuàn Rénmínbì de duìhuànlǜ shì duōshao?** 今天日元兑换人民币的兑换率是多少？
What's today's exchange rate for the Australian dollar to Chinese yuan?	**Jīntiān Àobì/Àoyuán duìhuàn Rénmínbì de duìhuànlǜ shì duōshao?** 今天澳币／澳元兑换人民币的兑换率是多少？

What's today's exchange rate for the Hong Kong dollar to Chinese yuan?	**Jīntiān Gǎngbì duìhuàn Rénmínbì de duìhuànlǜ shì duōshao?** 今天港币兑换人民币的兑换率是多少？
Can I withdraw money on my credit card here?	**Kěyǐ zài zhèlǐ yòng xìnyòngkǎ qǔqián ma?** 可以在这里用信用卡取钱吗？
What's the maximum amount?	**Yí cì zuìduō kěyǐ qǔ duōshao qián?** 一次最多可以取多少钱？
What's the minimum amount?	**Yí cì zuìshǎo kěyǐ qǔ duōshao qián?** 一次最少可以取多少钱？
I had some money cabled here.	**Yǒu rén gěi wǒ diànhuìle yìdiǎn qián lái.** 有人给我电汇了一点钱来。
These are the details of my bank in the US.	**Zhè shì wǒ zài Měiguó de yínháng zīliào.** 这是我在美国的银行资料。
This is the number of my bank account.	**Zhè shì wǒ de yínháng zhànghào.** 这是我的银行账号。
I'd like to change some money.	**Wǒ yào duìhuàn wàibì.** 我要兑换外币。
Could you give me some small change with it?	**Qǐng gěi wǒ yìxiē língqián.** 请给我一些零钱。
This is not right.	**Zhè ge búduì.** 这个不对。

请签名。 **Qǐng qiānmíng.**	Sign here, please.
请填这张表。 **Qǐng tián zhè zhāng biǎo.**	Fill this out, please.
请给我看看你的护照。 **Qǐng gěi wǒ kànkan nǐde hùzhào.**	Could I see your passport, please?
请给我看看你的身份证。 **Qǐng gěi wǒ kànkan nǐde shēnfènzhèng.**	Could I see your identity card, please?
请给我看看你的信用卡。 **Qǐng gěi wǒ kànkan nǐde xìnyòngkǎ.**	Could I see your credit card, please?

Could I have the bill, please?	**Qǐng gěi wǒ zhàngdān.** 请给我账单。
Could you put it on my bill?	**Qǐng jì zài wǒde zhàngdān shàng.** 请记在我的账单上。
Is everything included?	**Dōu suànjìnqu le ma?** 都算进去了吗？
Is the tip included?	**Xiǎofèi yě bāokuò le ma?** 小费也包括了吗？
Can I pay by credit card?	**Wǒ kěyǐ yòng xìnyòngkǎ fùkuǎn ma?** 我可以用信用卡付款吗？
Can I pay with foreign currency?	**Wǒ kěyǐ yòng wàibì fùkuǎn ma?** 我可以用外币付款吗？
You've given me too much change.	**Nǐ zhǎo gěi wǒ de qián tài duō le.** 你找给我的钱太多了。
You've given me not enough change.	**Nǐ zhǎo gěi wǒ de qián bú gòu.** 你找给我的钱不够。
Could you check this again, please?	**Qǐng nǐ zài suànyisuàn.** 请你再算一算。
Could I have a receipt, please?	**Qǐng gěi wǒ shōujù.** 请给我收据。
Keep the change.	**Búyòng zhǎo le.** 不用找了。

对不起，我们不接受信用卡。 **Duìbùqǐ, wǒmen bù jiē shòu xìnyòngkǎ.**	Sorry, we don't accept credit cards.
我们不接受旅行支票。 **Wǒmen bù jiē shòu lǚxíng zhīpiào.**	We don't accept traveler's checks.
我们不接受外币。 **Wǒmen bù jiē shòu lǚxíng wàibì.**	We don't accept foreign currency.

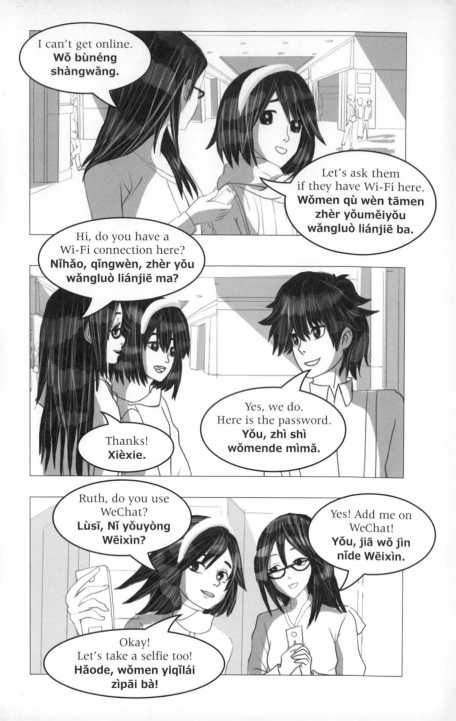

9. Mail, Phone and Internet

9.1 **Mail**
9.2 **Telephone**
9.3 **Internet/email**

 Mail

Post offices are open Monday to Saturday from 8:30 a.m. to 6 p.m. In fact, some post offices stay open until 9 p.m. although the range of services decreases towards late evening. The opening hours for Sundays are from 8:30 a.m. to 6 p.m. The cost of sending a letter depends on its weight, thus the long queues for weighing letters and buying stamps.

stamps **yóupiào** 邮票	money orders **diànhuì/(yóuzhèng/ yínháng) huìpiào** 电汇/(邮政／银行)汇票	postcard **míngxìnpiàn** 明信片	insured mail/ post **bǎojià yóujiàn** 保价邮件
parcels **bāoguǒ** 包裹	registered mail **guàhào yóujiàn** 挂号邮件	express mail **kuàidì** 快递	

Where is the nearest post office?	**Zuìjìn de yóujú zài nǎr/nǎli?** 最近的邮局在哪儿／哪里？
Where is the main post office?	**Yóujú zǒngjú zài nǎr/nǎli?** 邮局总局在哪儿／哪里？
Where is the nearest mail box?	**Zuìjìnde yóuxiāng zài nǎr/nǎli?** 最近的邮箱在哪儿／哪里？
Which counter should I go to to send a fax?	**Wǒ yīnggāi qù nǎ ge guìtái fā chuánzhēn?** 我应该去哪个柜台发传真？
Which counter should I go to wire a money order?	**Wǒ yīnggāi qù nǎ ge guìtái fā diànhuì?** 我应该去哪个柜台发电汇？
Which counter should I go to for general delivery?	**Wǒ yīnggāi qù nǎ ge guìtái qǔ yóujiàn?** 我应该去哪个柜台取邮件？

Is there any mail for me? **Yǒu méiyǒu wǒde xìn?** 有没有我的信？

Stamps

What's the postage for
  a letter to America?

**Jì xìn dào Měiguǒ de yóufèi shì
duōshao?** 寄信到美国的邮费是多少？

What's the postage for
  a postcard to America?

**Míngxìnpiàn dào Měiguǒ de yóufèi shì
duōshao?** 明信片到美国的邮费是多少？

Are there enough
  stamps on it?

Yóupiào gòu bu gòu? 邮票够不够？

I'd like two 10 RMB
  stamps.

**Wǒ yào liáng zhāng shíkuàiqián de
yóupiào.** 我要两张十块钱的邮票。

I'd like to send this letter
  by express mail.

Wǒ xiǎng yòng kuàiyóu jì zhège xìn.
我想用快邮寄这个信。

I'd like to send this letter
  by air mail.

Wǒ xiǎng yòng hángkōng jì zhège xìn.
我想用航空寄这个信。

I'd like to send this letter
  by registered mail.

Wǒ xiǎng yòng guàhào jì zhège xìn.
我想用挂号寄这个信。

I'd like to send this letter
  by surface mail.

Wǒ xiǎng yòng hǎiyùn jì zhège xìn.
我想用海运寄这个信。

Courier packages

I'd like to send a
  courier package.

Wǒ xiǎng fāsòng kuàidìbāo.
我想发送快递包。

Which counter should I
  go to send a
  courier package?

**Wǒ yīnggāi qù nǎ ge guìtái fāsòng
kuàidìbāo?**
我应该去哪个柜台发送快递包？

Can you help me send
  this package by courier?

Qǐng bāng wǒ fāsòng zhège kuàidìbāo.
请帮我发送这个快递包。

What is the cost? **Duōshao qián?** 多少钱？

9.2 Telephone

To call local numbers, you'll need either a local or international
data SIM card. The former can be obtained from most interna-

tional airports once you land. If your phone can work on the 900 or 1,800hz frequencies, you won't need to rent a local phone. To make local calls, dial 0, followed by the area code and the number for landlines. For mobile phone numbers, simply call the mobile phone number.

For international calls, dial 00, then the relevant country code (e.g., USA 1, Australia 61, UK 44), city code and number. If you need telephone assistance call 114, all operators speak English. Alternatively, save money by making voice and video calls through the various messaging apps, preferably using a fast Wi-Fi connection.

Is there a phone booth around here?	**Fùjìn yǒu gōngyòng diànhuàtíng ma?** 附近有公用电话亭吗？
Do you have a (city/regional) phone directory?	**Yǒu méiyǒu (běnshì/běnqū) de diànhuàbù?** 有没有（本市／本区）的电话簿？
Where can I get a phone card?	**Nǎli kěyǐ mǎi diànhuàkǎ?** 哪里可以买电话卡？
Could you connect me to room number 602?	**Qǐng bāng wǒ liánjiē dào liù líng èr hào fángjiān.** 请帮我连接到六零二号房间。
Could you give me the international access code?	**Qǐng gěi wǒ guójì chángtú de hàomǎ.** 请给我国际电话服务处的号码。
Could you give me the country code for the UK?	**Qǐng gěi wǒ Yīngguó de guójiā dàihào.** 请给我英国的国家代号。
Could you give me Beijing's area code?	**Qǐng gěi wǒ Běijīng de dìqūhào.** 请给我北京的地区号。
Can I dial international (long distance) direct?	**Wǒ kěyǐ zhíjiē dǎ guójì chángtú ma?** 我可以直接打国际长途吗？
Could you dial this number for me, please?	**Qǐng gěi wǒ dǎ zhè ge diànhuà hàomǎ.** 请给我打这个电话号码。
I'd like to place a long-distance collect call.	**Wǒ xiǎng dìng yí gè chángtú diànhuà, yào duìfāng fùkuǎn de.** 我想订一个长途电话，要对方付款的。

The conversation

Hello, this is…	**Wéi, zhè shì…** 喂，这是…
Who is this, please?	**Qǐngwèn, nín shì shéi?** 请问，您是谁?
Is this…?	**Nǐ shì…ma?** 你是…吗?
I'm sorry, I've dialed the wrong number.	**Duìbuqǐ, wǒ dǎcuò le.** 对不起，我打错了。
I can't hear you.	**Wǒ tīng bu qīngchu.** 我听不清楚。
I'd like to speak to…	**Wǒ zhǎo…** 我找…
Is…around?	**…Zài bu zài?** …在不在?
Do you speak English?	**Nǐ huì jiǎng Yīngyǔ ma?** 你会讲英语吗?
Extension…, please.	**Qǐng jiē…fēnjī.** 请接…分机。

你有电话。 **Nǐ yǒu diànhuà.**	There's a phone call for you.
你要先拨"零"。 **Nǐ yào xiān bō "líng".**	You have to dial "0" first.
请等一等。 **Qǐng děng yì děng.**	One moment, please.
没人接。 **Méi rén jiē.**	There's no answer.
电话占线。 **Diànhuà zhànxiàn.**	The line's busy.
您要等一下吗? **Nín yào děng yíxià ma?**	Do you want to hold?
你打错了。 **Nǐ dǎ cuòle.**	You've got a wrong number.
他不在。 他…点回来。 **Tā bù zài. Tā…diǎn huílái.**	He's not here right now. He'll be back at…
她不在。她…点回来。 **Tā bù zài. Tā…diǎn huílái.**	She's not here right now. She'll be back at…

Mail, Phone and Internet

9

Could you ask him to call me back?	**Qǐng ràng tā gěi wǒ huí ge diànhuà.** 请让他给我回个电话。
Could you ask her to call me back?	**Qǐng ràng tā gěi wǒ huí ge diànhuà.** 请让她给我回个电话。
My name's…	**Wǒ jiào…** 我叫…
My number's…	**Wǒ de diànhuà hàomǎ shì…** 我的电话号码是…
Could you tell him I called?	**Qǐng gàosu tā wǒ gěi tā dǎguo diànhuà.** 请告诉他我给他打过电话。
Could you tell her I called?	**Qǐng gàosu tā wǒ gěi tā dǎguo diànhuà.** 请告诉她我给她打过电话。
I'll call him back tomorrow.	**Wǒ míngtiān zài gěi tā huí diànhuà.** 我明天再给他回电话。
I'll call her back tomorrow.	**Wǒ míngtiān zài gěi tā huí diànhuà.** 我明天再给她回电话。

9.3 Internet/email

China is becoming increasingly connected, and free Wi-Fi is available in most restaurants, hotels and cafés in the larger cities, although the speed may be slow. Be sure to download several alternatives for the apps you will need, e.g., Apple or Baidu Maps instead of Google Maps.

Internet café **wǎngbā** 网吧	email **diànzǐyóujiàn** 电子邮件	blog **bókè** 博客	app (application) **yìngyòng chéngxù** 应用程序
social media **shèjiāo méitǐ** 社交媒体	e-book **diànzǐshū** 电子书	Weibo **Wēibó** 微博	instant messenger **liáotiān ruǎnjiàn** 聊天软件
portable power **yídòng diànyuán** 移动电源	Baidu **Bǎidù** 百度	Wechat **Wēixìn** 微信	Wi-Fi router **wúxiàn lùyóuqì** 无限路由器

Is there free Wi-Fi here? | **Zhèr yǒu miánfèide wǎngluò liánjiē ma?**
这儿有免费的网络链接吗?

What is your email address? | **Nǐ de diànzǐyóujiàn dìzhǐ shì shénme?**
你的电子邮件地址是什么?

My email address is... | **Wǒde diànzǐyóujiàn dìzhǐ shì...**
我的电子邮件地址是…

Could you send me an email? | **Kěyǐ qǐng nǐ fā diànzǐyóujiàn gěi wǒ ma?** 可以请你发电子邮件给我吗?

I will get back to you via email. | **Wǒ huì fā diànzǐyóujiàn huífù nǐ.**
我会发电子邮件回复你。

The Internet connection is unstable. | **Wǎngluò liánjiē bùwěndìng.**
网络连接不稳定。

The Internet connection is slow. | **Wǎngluò liánjiē hěnmàn.**
网络连接很慢。

Can I borrow a Wi-Fi router? | **Néng jièyòng yíxià wǔxiàn lùyóuqì ma?**
能借用一下无线路由器吗?

Can I borrow a portable charger? | **Néng jièyòng yíxià yídòng diànyuán ma?**
能借用一下移动电源吗?

Let's take a selfie. | **Wǒmen zìpāi yīzhāng ba.**
我们自拍一张吧。

Add me on WeChat. | **Jiā wǒ Wēixìn ba.** 加我微信吧。

I will send you the picture via WeChat. | **Wǒ huì tōngguò Wēixìn bǎ zhàopiàn chuán gěinǐ.**
我会通过微信把照片传给你。

I have uploaded our photos on WeChat. | **Wǒ yǐjīng bǎ wǒmen de zhàopiàn shàngchuán dào Wēixìn.**
我已经把我们的照片上传到微信。

Do you have a WeChat account? | **Nǐ yǒu Wēixìn zhànghào ma?**
你有微信账号吗?

Can I add you on WeChat? | **Wǒ néng jiā nǐ Wēixìn ma?**
我能加你微信吗?

What is your mobile phone number?	**Nǐ de shǒujī hàomǎ shì shénme?** 你的手机号码是什么？
What is your Weibo ID?	**Nǐ de Wēibó míngchēng shì shénme?** 你的微博名称是什么？
Can I follow you on Weibo?	**Wǒ néng zài Wēibó shàng guānzhù nǐ ma?** 我能在微博上关注你吗？
Can I put our photos on my Weibo?	**Wǒ néng bǎ wǒmen de zhàopiàn fàngdào Wēibó shàng ma?** 我能把我们的照片放到微博上吗？
Do you have this translation app?	**Nǐ yǒu zhègè fānyì yìngyòng ma?** 你有这个翻译应用吗？
Do you have this game app?	**Nǐ yǒu zhègè yóuxì yìngyòng ma?** 你有这个游戏应用吗？
Do you have this train ticket booking app?	**Nǐ yǒu zhègè lièchēpiào yùdìng yìngyòng ma?** 你有这个列车票预订应用吗？
Do you have this hotel booking app?	**Nǐ yǒu zhègè jiǔdiàn yùdìng yìngyòng ma?** 你有这个游戏应用吗？
Do you have a printer here?	**Zhèlǐ yǒu dǎyìngjī ma?** 这里有打印机吗？
How much would it cost to print one sheet of paper in black and white?	**Dǎyìng yīzhāng hēibái de duōshǎo qián?** 打印一张黑白的多少钱？
It's my ticket confirmation.	**Zhè shì wǒ de jīpiào quèrènhán.** 这是我的机票确认函。
It's my hotel reservation.	**Zhè shì wǒ de jiǔdiàn yùdìng quèrènhán.** 这是我的酒店预订确认函。
It's my boarding pass.	**Zhè shì wǒ de dēngjīpái.** 这是我的登机牌。
It's my travel itinerary.	**Zhè shì wǒ de xíngchéngdān.** 这是我的行程单。

10. Shopping

Most shops in China are open seven days a week. Corner shops are open from 8:30 a.m. till 10 p.m. Supermarkets are open from 8:30 a.m. till 8:30 p.m., some places up to 9 p.m. Department stores are open from 9 or 10 a.m. till 9 p.m., while some places are open up to 10 p.m.

supermarket
chāo (jí) shì (chǎng)
超(级)市(场)

department store
bǎihuò gōngsī
百货公司

fruit and vegetable shop
shuǐguǒ shūcàidiàn
水果蔬菜店

grocery shop
záhuòdiàn
杂货店

florist
huādiàn
花店

market
shìchǎng
市场

fishmonger
yúdiàn
鱼店

household goods
jiātíng yòngpǐn diàn
家庭用品店

household appliances
jiāyòng diànqìdiàn
家用电器店

household linen shop
chuángdān zhuōbùdiàn
床单桌布店

watches and clocks
zhōngbiáodiàn
钟表店

optician
yǎnjìngshāng
眼镜商

clothing shop
fúzhuāngdiàn
服装店

ice-cream stand
**bīngjīlíngdiàn/
bīngqílíndiàn**
冰激凌店／冰淇淋店

music shop (CDs,
DVDs, etc)
yīnxiàngdiàn
音像店

barber
lǐfàdiàn
理发店

hairdresser
lǐfàshī/lǐfàdiàn
理发师／理发店

perfumery
xiāngshuǐdiàn
香水店

leather goods
pígé yòngpǐn (diàn)
皮革用品(店)

Chinese medicine
shop
zhōngyàodiàn
中药店

goldsmith
jīnshìgōng
金饰工

toy shop
wánjùdiàn
玩具店

jeweler
zhūbǎoshāng
珠宝商

beauty salon
měiróngdiàn
美容店

laundry/coin-operated
  laundry/dry cleaner
**xǐyīdiàn/tóu bì xǐyīdiàn/
  gānxǐdiàn**
洗衣店/投币洗衣店/干
洗店

baker's shop
miànbāodiàn
面包店

cobbler
xiūxiédiàn
修鞋店

camera shop
zhàoxiàngjīdiàn
照相机店

stationery shop
wénjùdiàn
文具店

sporting goods
**yùndòng yòngpǐn
  (diàn)**
运动用品(店)

bookshop
shūdiàn
书店

confectioner's/cake
  shop
**tángguǒdiàn/
  gāodiǎndiàn**
糖果店/糕点店

motorbike/moped/
  bicycle repairs
**mótuōchē/
  zhùdòngchē/
  zìxíngchē
  wéixiūdiàn**
摩托车/助动车/
自行车维修店

pharmacy
yàodiàn
药店

newsstand
bàotíng
报亭

delicatessen
shúshídiàn
熟食店

10.1 Shopping conversations

Where can I get…?

Nǎli kěyǐ mǎidào...?　哪里可以买到…?

When is this shop open?

Zhè jiā shāngdiàn jǐdiǎn kāimén?
这家商店几点开门?

Could you tell me where
  the…department is?

Bùhǎoyìsi, ...bùmén zài nǎli?
不好意思,…部门在哪里?

Could you help me,
  please?

Bùhǎoyìsi, néng máfan nǐ yíxià ma?
不好意思,能麻烦你一下吗?

I'm looking for…

Wǒ zhǎo...　我找…

Do you sell English
  language newspapers?

Nǐmen yǒu Yīngwén bàozhǐ ma?
你们有英文报纸吗?

你有人招呼了吗?
Nǐ yǒurén zhāohū le ma?

Are you being served?

No, I'd like…   **Hái méiyǒu, wǒ xiǎng mǎi...**
                                 还没有，我想买…

I'm just looking, if   **Wǒ zhǐshì kànkan, kěyǐ ma?**
that's all right.   我只是看看，可以吗？

还要别的吗？
Hái yào bié de ma?   (Would you like) anything else?

Yes, I'd also like…   **Wǒ hái yào...** 我还要…

No, thank you. That's all.   **Búyòng le, xièxie.** 不用了，谢谢。

Could you show me…?   **Qǐng ná...gěi wǒ kànkan.**
                                 请拿…给我看看。

I'd prefer…   **Wǒ xǐhuan...** 我喜欢…

This is not what I'm   **Zhè búshì wǒ yào de.**
looking for.   这不是我要的。

Thank you, I'll keep   **Méiguānxi, wǒ zài kànkan.**
looking.   没关系，我再看看。

Do you have something   **Yǒu méiyǒu piányi yì diǎnr de?**
less expensive?   有没有便宜一点儿的？

Do you have something   **Yǒu méiyǒu xiǎo yì diǎnr de?**
smaller?   有没有小一点儿的？

Do you have something   **Yǒu méiyǒu dà yì diǎnr de?**
larger?   有没有大一点儿的？

I'll take this one.   **Wǒ jiù yào zhè ge.** 我就要这个。

Does it come with   **Yǒu méiyǒu shuōmíngshū?**
instructions?   有没有说明书？

It's too expensive.   **Tài guì le.** 太贵了。

I'll give you…   **Wǒ chū...kuàiqián, zěnmeyàng?**
                                 我出…块钱，怎么样？

Could you keep this   **Qǐng tì wǒ liúzhe zhè ge.**
for me?   请替我留着这个。

131

I'll come back for it later. **Wǒ yìhuǐr zài lái mǎi.**
我一会儿再来买。

Do you have a bag for me, please? **Qǐng gěi wǒ yí ge dàizi.**
请给我一个袋子。

Could you gift-wrap it, please? **Qǐng gěi wǒ bāochéng lǐwù.**
请给我包成礼物。

对不起，我们没有这种。 I'm sorry, we don't have this.
Duìbuqǐ, wǒmen méiyǒu zhè zhǒng.

对不起，都卖完了。 I'm sorry, we're sold out.
Duìbuqǐ, dōu mài wánle.

对不起，要等到…才有货。 I'm sorry, it won't come in until…
Duìbuqǐ, yào děngdào...cái yǒu huò.

请到付款台结账。 Please pay at the cash register.
Qǐng dào fùkuǎntái jiézhàng.

我们不接受信用卡。 We don't accept credit cards.
Wǒmen bù jiēshòu xìnyòngkǎ.

我们不接受旅行支票。 We don't accept traveler's checks.
Wǒmen bù jiēshòu lǚxíng zhīpiào.

10.2 Food

I'd like half a kilo of beef. **Wǒ yào bàn gōngjīn niúròu.**
我要半公斤牛肉。

I'd like a kilo of chicken. **Wǒ yào yī gōngjīn jīròu.**
我要一公斤鸡肉。

Could you cut it up for me, please? **Qǐng bāng wǒ qiēkāi.** 请帮我切开。

Can I order it? **Wǒ kěyǐ dìnggòu ma?** 我可以订购吗？

I'll pick it up tomorrow at… **Wǒ míngtiān...lái qǔ.** 我明天…来取。

Can you eat this? **Zhè ge kěyǐ chī ma?** 这个可以吃吗？

| Can you drink this? | **Zhè ge kěyǐ hē ma?** 这个可以喝吗？ |
| What's in it? | **Lǐmiàn yǒu shénme?** 里面有什么？ |

10.3 Clothing and shoes

I'd like something to go with this.	**Yǒu méiyǒu shénme pèi zhè ge de?** 有没有什么配这个的？
Do you have shoes to match this?	**Yǒu méiyǒu pèi zhè ge de xié?** 有没有配这个的鞋？
I'm a size…in the U.S.	**Wǒ chuān (Měiguó)…hào de.** 我穿（美国）…号的。
Can I try this on?	**Wǒ kěyǐ shìchuān ma?** 我可以试穿吗？
Where's the fitting room?	**Shìyīshì zài nǎlǐ?** 试衣室在哪里？
It doesn't suit me.	**Zhè bù hé wǒ chuān.** 这件不合我穿。
This is the right size.	**Zhège dàxiǎo zhènghǎo.** 这个大小正好。
It doesn't look good on me.	**Wǒ chuānqǐlái bù hǎokàn.** 我穿起来不好看。
Do you have these in white?	**Zhèxiē yǒu méiyǒu báisè de?** 这些有没有白色的？
Do you have these in black?	**Zhèxiē yǒu méiyǒu hēisè de?** 这些有没有黑色的？
Do you have these in green?	**Zhèxiē yǒu méiyǒu lǜsè de?** 这些有没有绿色的？
Do you have these in red?	**Zhèxiē yǒu méiyǒu hóngsè de?** 这些有没有红色的？
Do you have these in blue?	**Zhèxiē yǒu méiyǒu lánsè de?** 这些有没有蓝色的？
The heel's too high.	**Xiégēn tài gāo le.** 鞋跟太高了。
The heel's too low.	**Xiégēn tài ǎi le.** 鞋跟太矮了。

Is this real leather?	**Zhè shì zhēn pí ma?** 这是真皮吗？
Is this genuine hide?	**Zhè shì zhēn shòupí ma?** 这是真兽皮吗？
I'm looking for a dress for a four-year-old child.	**Wǒ zhǎo yí (ge)liányīqún sòng gěi sì suì xiǎohái.** 我找一（个）连衣裙送给四岁小孩。
I'd like a silk blouse.	**Wǒ yào yí jiàn zhēnsī de nǚ chènshān.** 我要一件真丝的女衬衫。
I'd like a cotton shirt.	**Wǒ yào yí jiàn miánbù de chènshān.** 我要一件棉布的衬衫。
I'd like a woolen jacket.	**Wǒ yào yí jiàn máoliào de.** 我要一件毛料的外套。
I'd like a pair of linen pants.	**Wǒ yào yí tiáo yàmábù de kùzi** 我要一条亚麻布的裤子。
At what temperature should I wash it?	**Wǒ yīnggāi yòng shénme shuǐwēn xǐ?** 我应该用什么水温洗？
Will it shrink in the wash?	**Huì suōshuǐ ma?** 会缩水吗？

Hand wash **Shǒuxǐ** 手洗	Do not spin dry. **Wù yòng shuǎigànjī gānzào.** 勿用甩干机干燥。	Do not iron. **Wù yòng yùndǒu yùn.** 勿用熨斗熨。
Dry clean **Gānxǐ** 干洗	Lay flat **Píng fàng** 平放	Machine washable **Kěyòng xǐyījī xǐ** 可用洗衣机洗

At the cobbler

Could you mend these shoes?	**Zhè shuāng xié kěyǐ xiūbǔ ma?** 这双鞋可以修补吗？
Could you resole these shoes?	**Zhè shuāng xié kěyǐ huàn dǐ ma?** 这双鞋可以换底吗？
When will they be ready?	**Shénme shíhou néng qǔ?** 什么时候能取？

I'd like a can of shoe polish, please.

Qǐng gěi wǒ yì hé xiéyóu.
请给我一盒鞋油。

I'd like a pair of shoe laces, please.

Qǐng gěi wǒ yì fù xiédài.
请给我一副鞋带。

10.4 At the hairdresser

Do I have to make an appointment?

Wǒ yào yùyuē ma? 我要预约吗?

Can I come in right now?

Wǒ kěyǐ xiànzài lái ma?
我可以现在来吗?

How long will I have to wait?

Yào děng duōjiǔ? 要等多久?

I'd like a shampoo.

Wǒ xiǎng xǐtóu. 我想洗头。

I'd like a haircut.

Wǒ xiǎng lǐfà. 我想理发。

I'd like a shampoo for oily hair, please.

Wǒ xiǎng xǐtóu. Wǒ de tóufa bǐjiào yóu.
我想洗头。我的头发比较油。

I'd like a shampoo for dry hair, please.

Wǒ xiǎng xǐtóu. Wǒ de tóufa bǐjiào gān.
我想洗头。我的头发比较干。

I'd like an anti-dandruff shampoo.

Wǒ yào qù tóupíxuè de xǐfàjì.
我要去头皮屑的洗发剂。

I'd like a color-rinse shampoo, please.

Wǒ yào bǎosè de xǐfàjì.
我要保色的洗发剂。

I'd like a shampoo with conditioner, please.

Wǒ yào dài hùfàsù de xǐfàjì.
我要带护发素的洗发剂。

I'd like highlights, please.

Qǐng gěi wǒ jiādiǎn xiǎnyǎn de yánsè.
请给我加点显眼的颜色。

Do you have a color chart, please?

Yǒu méiyǒu sèpǔ? 有没有色谱?

I'd like to keep the same color.

Wǒ xiǎng bǎochí tóngyàng de yánsè.
我想保持同样的颜色。

135

I'd like it darker.	**Wǒ yào sè shēn yìdiǎn.** 我要色深一点。
I'd like it lighter.	**Wǒ yào sè qiǎn yìdiǎn.** 我要色浅一点。
I'd like hairspray.	**Qǐng gěi wǒ pēn dìngxíngjiāo.** 请给我喷定型胶。
I don't want hairspray.	**Qǐng búyào gěi wǒ pēn dìngxíngjiāo.** 请不要给我喷定型胶。
I'd like gel.	**Qǐng gěi wǒ fàlà.** 请给我发蜡。
I don't want lotion.	**Qǐng búyào gěi wǒ xǐfàlù/yíngyǎngjì.** 请不要给我洗发露／营养剂。
I'd like short bangs.	**Wǒ yào duǎn yìdiǎn de liúhǎir.** 我要短一点的刘海儿。
Not too short at the back	**Hòumiàn de tóufà qǐng búyào jiǎnde tài duǎn.** 后面的头发请不要剪得太短。
Not too long	**Búyào tài cháng** 不要太长
I'd like it curly.	**Wǒ yào tàng juǎnfà.** 我要烫卷发。
I don't like it too curly.	**Wǒ búyào tàng de tài juǎn.** 我不要烫得太卷。
It needs a little taken off.	**Wǒ xūyào xuēbáo yìdiǎn.** 我需要削薄一点。
It needs a lot taken off.	**Wǒ xūyào xuēbáo hěnduō.** 我需要削薄很多。
I'd like a completely different style.	**Wǒ yào jiǎn yí ge wánquán bùtóng de fàxíng.** 我要剪一个完全不同的发型。
I'd like it the same as in this photo.	**Wǒ yào jiǎn xiàng zhè zhāng zhàopiàn yíyàng de fàxíng.** 我要剪像这张照片一样的发型。
I'd like it the same as that woman's.	**Wǒ yào jiǎn xiàng zhè wèi nǚshì yíyàng de fàxíng.** 我要剪像这位女士一样的发型。

Could you turn the drier up a bit?	**Qǐng bǎ chuīfēngjī tiáogāo yìdiǎn.** 请把吹风机调高一点。
Could you turn the drier down a bit?	**Qǐng bǎ chuīfēngjī tiáodī yìdiǎn.** 请把吹风机调低一点。
I'd like a facial.	**Wǒ xiǎng zuò yí ge miànmò.** 我想做一个面膜。
I'd like a manicure.	**Wǒ xiǎng xiū zhījiǎ.** 我想修指甲。
Could you trim my bangs please?	**Qǐng gěi wǒ xiū yíxià liúhǎir.** 请给我修一下刘海儿。
Could you trim my beard please?	**Qǐng gěi wǒ xiū yíxià húxū.** 请给我修一下胡须。
Could you trim my moustache please?	**Qǐng gěi wǒ xiū yíxià xiǎohúzi.** 请给我修一下小胡子。
I'd like a shave, please.	**Qǐng gěi wǒ guāgua húzi.** 请给我刮刮胡子。

你想剪什么发型? **Nǐ xiǎng jiǎn shénme fàxíng?**	What style did you have in mind?
你想染成什么颜色? **Nǐ xiǎng rǎn chéng shénme yánsè?**	What color did you want it?
温度合适吗? **Wēndù héshì ma?**	Is the temperature all right for you?
你想看什么杂志吗? **Nǐ xiǎng kàn shénme zázhì ma?**	Would you like something to read?
你想喝点饮料吗? **Nǐ xiǎng hē diǎn yǐnliào ma?**	Would you like a drink?

11. Tourist Activities

The China National Tourism Administration (CNTA) is a government organization that promotes and looks after the tourism industry of China. It has 15 international overseas offices, including those in U.S., Canada, Australia and Asia. Its website (www.cnta.gov.cn) provides lots of information for tourists going to China. Other useful websites include TripAdvisor and Lonely Planet etc.

Most travelers arrive with a pre-arranged package from overseas agencies which are generally affiliated with two semi-government travel agencies in China—China International Travel Service, and China Travel Service. Both have branches in major cities and towns. In addition there are private travel agents such as the China Youth Travel Service which cater to individual travelers. All travel agencies mainly advise on tours and package deals with the flexibility of car hire (with driver) and personal guides. These offices are generally open every day.

If you intend to travel independently, do your research beforehand, and book what you can online prior to your trip. It may be useful also to download a map application such as Baidu and rent a pocket Wi-Fi router. Have your hotel concierge write down (in Chinese characters) the places you want to go to, so you can show them to the bus driver, train staff or taxi driver.

11.1 Sightseeing

Places to Visit

Beijing, China's capital, is the second largest city. It is the center of commerce and trade on Mainland China. The top places to visit in Beijing are:

- The **Palace Museum** (故宫 **Gùgōng**). The palace was built between 1406 and 1420, but was burnt down, rebuilt, and renovated several times. Admission is 40 RMB. Open from 8.30 a.m. to 4.30 p.m.

- The **Temple of Heaven** (天坛 **Tiāntán**). It was initially built in 1420, covering an area of 273 hectares. In 1998, it was designated as a UNESCO World Heritage Site; admission is 15 RMB, open from 6 a.m. to 10 p.m.

- The **Summer Palace** (颐和园 **Yíhéyuán**); admission is 30 RMB. Opens from 6.30 a.m. to 6 p.m.

- **Beijing National Stadium**, also known as the Bird's Nest (鸟巢 **Niǎocháo**), designed for use throughout the 2008 Summer Olympics and Paralympics, and open to visitors from 9 a.m. to 9 p.m.

Shanghai has lots to offer both first-timers and repeat visitors—from museums, cinemas, and arts to fashion. The famous places to visit in Shanghai are:

- The **Shanghai Museum** (上海博物馆 **Shànghǎi Bówùguǎn**), a museum of ancient Chinese art, situated on the People's Square (人民广场 **Rénmín Guǎngchǎng**); open to the public 9 a.m. to 5 p.m.

- **Shanghai World Financial Center** (上海环球金融中心 **Shànghǎi Huánqiú Jīnróng Zhōngxīn**), consisting of offices, hotels, conference rooms, observation desks and shopping malls on the ground floors; open daily from 8 a.m. to 11 p.m.

- The **Oriental Pearl Radio & TV Tower** (东方明珠 **Dōngfāng Míngzhū**). It's one of the most famous landmarks in Shanghai, and is open daily from 8 a.m. to 9.30 p.m.

Hong Kong, a British colony until 1997, is known for its expansive skyline and deep natural harbor and is one of the most densely populated areas in the world. The places to visit are:

- **Avenue of Stars** (星光大道 **Xīngguāng Dàdào**), where you can see stunning views of the harbor tower, while the names of Hong Kong's movie icons lie beneath your feet.
- **The Peak** (太平山 **Tàipíngshān**); the mountain is located in the western half of Hong Kong Island where you can see the Victoria Harbor and the city. It is open from 7 a.m. to 12 a.m.

More information about the top attractions in China can be found from the website: http://en.cnta.gov.cn/TravelInChina. Other popular sites are listed in the box below.

The Bund **Wàitān** 外滩	Forbidden City **Zǐjīnchéng** 紫禁城	Tian'anmen Square **Tiān'ānmén Guǎngchǎng** 天安门广场
Terracotta Army **Bīngmǎyǒng** 兵马俑	Yellow River **Huánghé** 黄河	Badaling (Great Wall) **Bādálǐng (Chángchéng)** 八达岭(长城)
Ladies' Market **Nǚrénjiē** 女人街	Jiuzhaigou Valley **Jiǔzhàigōu** 九寨沟	Hanshan Temple **Hánshānsì** 寒山寺

11.2 Places of interest

Where's the Tourist Information, please?	**Qǐngwèn, lǚyóu zīxúntái zài nǎli?** 请问，旅游资询台在哪里？
Do you have a city map?	**Yǒu běnshì dìtú ma?** 有本市地图吗？
Where is the museum?	**Bówùguǎn zài nǎli?** 博物馆在哪里？
Where can I find a church?	**Nǎlǐ yǒu jiàotáng?** 哪里有教堂？
Could you give me some information about...?	**Nǐ kěyǐ gěi wǒ yǒuguān...de zīliào ma?** 你可以给我有关…的资料吗？
How much is this?	**Zhè ge duōshao qián?** 这个多少钱？

What are the main places of interest?	**Zhǔyào yóuwán de dìfāng yǒu nǎxiē?** 主要游玩的地方有哪些？
Could you point them out on the map?	**Qǐng zài dìtú shàng zhǐ gěi wǒ kànkan.** 请在地图上指给我看看。
What do you recommend?	**Nǐ tuījiàn nǎ ge jǐngdiǎn?** 你推荐哪个景点？
We'll be here for a few hours.	**Wǒmen yào zài zhèlǐ dāi jǐ ge xiǎoshí.** 我们要在这里呆几个小时。
We'll be here for a day.	**Wǒmen yào zài zhèlǐ dāi yìtiān.** 我们要在这里呆一天。
We'll be here for a week.	**Wǒmen yào zài zhèlǐ dāi yí ge xīngqí.** 我们要在这里呆一个星期。
We're interested in…	**Wǒmen duì…gǎn xìngqù** 我们对…感兴趣
How long does it take?	**Yào zǒu duōjiǔ?** 要走多久？
Where does it start?	**Zài nǎli kāishǐ?** 在哪里开始？
Where does it end?	**Zài nǎli jiéshù?** 在哪里结束？
Are there any boat trips?	**Yǒu méiyǒu zuòchuán de lǚyóu hángxiàn?** 有没有坐船的旅游航线？
Where can we board?	**Zài nǎli shàngchuán?** 在哪里上船？
Are there any bus tours?	**Yǒu méiyǒu zuò lǚyóuchē de lùxiàn?** 有没有坐旅游车的路线？
Where do we get on?	**Zài nǎli shàngchē?** 在哪里上车？
Is there a guide who speaks English?	**Yǒu méiyǒu dǎoyóu huì shuō Yīngyǔ de?** 有没有导游会说英语的？
What trips can we take around the area?	**Fùjìn yǒu shénme jǐngdiǎn zhídé qù wán de?** 附近有什么景点值得去玩的？
Are there any excursions?	**Yǒu méiyǒu duǎntú lǚyóu lùxiàn?** 有没有短途旅游路线？
Where do they go?	**Zhèxiē duǎntú lǚyóu qù nǎli?** 这些短途旅游去哪里？

How long is the excursion?	**Zhè ge duǎntú lǚyóu yǒu duō yuǎn?** 这个短途旅游有多远？
We'd like to go to the Palace Museum.	**Wǒmen xiǎng qù Gùgōng.** 我们想去故宫。
We'd like to go to the Forbidden City.	**Wǒmen xiǎng qù Zǐjìnchéng.** 我们想去紫禁城。
We'd like to go to the Shanghai Museum.	**Wǒmen xiǎng qù Shànghǎi bówùguǎn.** 我们想去上海博物馆。
How much does it cost to...?	**Dào...duōshao qián?** 到…多少钱？
How much is the admission ticket?	**Ménpiào duōshao qián?** 门票多少钱？
How long do we stay in…?	**Wǒmen zài...dāi duōjiǔ?** 我们在…呆多久？
Are there any guided tours?	**Zhèxiē lǚyóutuán yǒu méiyǒu dǎoyóu?** 这些旅游团有没有导游？
Do you have an English tour?	**Yǒu méiyǒu Yīngyǔ jiǎngjiě fúwù?** 有没有英语讲解服务？
How much free time will we have there?	**Dàole nàli, wǒmen yǒu duōshao zìyóu huódòng shíjiān?** 到了那里，我们有多少自由活动时间？
We want to have a walk around.	**Wǒmen xiǎng zài fùjìn zǒuzou.** 我们想在附近走走。
Can we hire a guide?	**Kěyǐ gùyòng yí ge dǎoyóu ma?** 可以雇用一个导游吗？
What time does... open?	**...jǐdiǎn kāimén?** …几点开门？
What time does... close?	**...jǐdiǎn guānmén?** …几点关门？
What days are... open?	**...nǎ tiān kāimén?** …哪天开门？
What days are... closed?	**...nǎ tiān guānmén?** …哪天关门？
What's the admission price?	**Rùchǎngfèi shì duōshǎo?** 入场费是多少？

Is there a group discount?	**Tuántǐ yǒu méiyǒu yōuhuì?**
	团体有没有优惠？
Is there a child discount?	**Xiǎohái yǒu méiyǒu yōuhuì?**
	小孩有没有优惠？
Is there a student discount?	**Xuěshēng yǒu méiyǒu yōuhuì?**
	学生有没有优惠？
Is there a discount for senior citizens?	**Lǎorén yǒu méiyǒu yōuhuì?**
	老人有没有优惠？
Can I take flash photos here?	**Zhèlǐ kěyǐ yòng shǎnguāngdēng zhàoxiàng ma?**
	这里可以用闪光灯照相吗？
Can I film here?	**Zhèlǐ kěyǐ pāi lùxiàng ma?**
	这里可以拍录像吗？
Do you have an English catalog?	**Yǒu méiyǒu Yīngwén de mùlù?**
	有没有英文的目录？
Do you have an English program?	**Yǒu méiyǒu Yīngwén de jiémùbiǎo?**
	有没有英文的节目表？
Do you have an English travel brochure?	**Yǒu méiyǒu Yīngwén de lǚyóushǒucè?**
	有没有英文的旅游手册？

11.3 Going out

China has an increasing number of bars, discos, late-night restaurants and coffee shops. In major cities there are various evening performances every night. Try to see a martial arts or acrobatic performance, a concert or Beijing opera.

Do you have this week's entertainment guide?	**Yǒu méiyǒu běnzhōu de yúlè zhǐ'nán?**
	有没有本周的娱乐指南？
Do you have this month's entertainment guide?	**Yǒu méiyǒu běnyuè de yúlè zhǐ'nán?**
	有没有本月的娱乐指南？
What's on tonight?	**Jīnwǎn yǒu shénme hǎo jiémù?**
	今晚有什么好节目？

We want to go to… **Wǒmen xiǎng qù…** 我们想去…

What's playing at the cinema? **Diànyǐngyuàn shàngyìng shénme?**
电影院上映什么?

What sort of film is that? **Nà shì shénme diànyǐng?**
那是什么电影?

This film is suitable for everyone. **Zhège diànyǐng dàrén xiǎohái dōu néng kàn.** 这个电影大人小孩都能看。

This film is not suitable for people under 16 years old. **Zhège diànyǐng shíliù suì yǐxià de értóng bùyí kàn.**
这个电影十六岁以下的儿童不宜看。

This film has subtitles. **Zhège diànyǐng yǒu zìmù de.**
这个电影有字幕的。

This film is dubbed. **Zhège diànyǐng fānyì pèiyīn de.**
这个电影翻译配音的。

What's on at the theater? **Xìjù yǒu shénme shàngyìng?**
戏剧有什么上映?

What's on at the opera? **Gējù yǒu shénme shàngyìng?**
歌剧有什么上映?

What's happening in the concert hall? **Yīnyuètīng yǒu shénme biǎoyǎn?**
音乐厅有什么表演?

Where can I find a good nightclub around here? **Fùjìn nǎli yǒu hǎo de yèzǒnghuì?**
附近哪里有好的夜总会?

Is there a cover charge for entry to this bar? **Zhège jiǔbā yǒuméiyǒu fēngmiànfèi?**
这个酒吧有没有封面费?

Is it evening wear only? **Yào chuān wǎnzhuāng ma?**
要穿晚装吗?

Is it Ladies' Night today? **Jīntiān shìbushì nǔshì zhī yè?**
今天是不是女士之夜?

What is your signature drink? **Nǐde zhāopái yǐnliào shi shénme?**
你的招牌饮料是什么?

Should I/we dress up? **Wǒ(men) yào chuānde zhèngshì ma?**
我(们)要穿得正式吗?

What time does the show start?	**Biǎoyǎn shénme shíhou kāiyǎn?** 表演什么时候开演？
Could you reserve some tickets for us?	**Qǐng gěi wǒmen yùdìng jǐ zhāng piào.** 请给我们预订几张票。
We'd like to book three seats.	**Wǒmen xiǎng dìng sānge rén de zuòr.** 我们想订三个人的座儿。
We'd like to book a table for three.	**Wǒmen xiǎng dìng sānge rén de zhuōzi.** 我们想订三个人的桌子。

1.4 Nightlife

Where's the bar?	**Jiǔbā zài nǎli?** 酒吧在哪里？
Is there a disco here?	**Zhèlǐ yǒu dísīkē ma?** 这里有迪斯科吗？
Please bring me a beer.	**Qǐng gěi wǒ lái yì bēi píjiǔ.** 请给我来一杯啤酒。
I'd like a glass of whisky, straight.	**Wǒ xiǎng yào yì bēi wēishìjì, bù jiā bīngkuài.** 我想要一杯威士忌，不加冰块。
I'd like a glass of whisky, on the rocks.	**Wǒ xiǎng yào yì bēi wēishìjì, jiā bīngkuài.** 我想要一杯威士忌，加冰块。

1.5 Cultural performances

Activities

Is there a cinema nearby?	**Zhè fùjìn nǎlǐ yǒu diànyǐngyuàn?** 这附近哪里有电影院？
Is there a tea house nearby?	**Zhè fùjìn nǎlǐ yǒu chálóu?** 这附近哪里有茶楼？
When does the gallery open and close?	**Huàláng jǐdiǎn kāimén, jǐdiǎn guānmén?** 画廊几点开门，几点关门？

concert	theater	spicy hotpot
yīnyuèhuì	**jùyuàn**	**málà huǒguō**
音乐会	剧院	麻辣火锅
acrobatics troupe	cinema	gallery
zájìtuán	**diànyǐngyuàn**	**huàláng**
杂技团	电影院	画廊
traditional market	museum	night view
chuántǒng shìjí	**bówùguǎn**	**yèjǐng**
传统市集	博物馆	夜景
dim sum	night market	
gǎngshì diǎnxīn	**yèshì**	
港式点心	夜市	

When does the museum open and close?
Bówùguǎn jǐdiǎn kāimén, jǐdiǎn guānmén?
博物馆几点开门，几点关门？

Where can I see...?
Nǎlǐ kéyǐ kàn...? 哪里可以看…？

Where can I eat...?
Nǎlǐ kéyǐ chī...? 哪里可以吃…？

I'd like to see Beijing Opera.
Wǒ xiǎng kàn Jīngjù.
我想看京剧。

I'd like to see face-changing in Sichuan Opera.
Wǒ xiǎng kàn Chuānjùbiànliǎn.
我想看川剧变脸。

I'd like to see an acrobatic performance.
Wǒ xiǎng kàn zájì biǎoyǎn.
我想看杂技表演。

I'd like to see a song-and-dance show.
Wǒ xiǎng kàn gēwǔ. 我想看歌舞。

I'd like to see a martial arts performance.
Wǒ xiǎng kàn wǔshù biǎoyǎn.
我想看武术表演。

I'd like to see a folk dance.
Wǒ xiǎng kàn mínjiān wǔdǎo.
我想看民间舞蹈。

I'd like to see a Chinese classical music concert.
Wǒ xiǎng kàn Zhōngguó mínyuè yǎnzòu. 我想看中国民乐演奏。

I'd like to go to a concert.
Wǒ xiǎng qù tīng yīnyuèhuì.
我想去听音乐会。

Are there English subtitles?	**Yǒu méiyǒu Yīngwén zìmù?** 有没有英文字幕？
Are there any tickets for tonight's show?	**Yǒu méiyǒu jīnwǎn de piào?** 有没有今晚的票？
How much are the least expensive seats?	**Zuì piányi de zuòwèi duōshao qián?** 最便宜的座位多少钱？
How much are front row seats?	**Qiánpái zuòwèi duōshao qián?** 前排座位多少钱？

11.6 Booking tickets

Could I reserve three seats for the eight o'clock performance?	**Wǒ xiǎng yùdìng sān zhāng bādiǎn kāiyǎn de piào.** 我想预订三张八点开演的票。
Could I reserve front row seats?	**Wǒ xiǎng yùdìng qiánpái de zuòr.** 我想预订前排的座儿。
Could I reserve a table for eight people at the front?	**Wǒ xiǎng yùdìng zài qiánmiàn de bā ge rén de zhuōzi** 我想预订在前面的八个人的桌子。
Could I reserve seats in the middle?	**Wǒ xiǎng yùdìng zhōngjiān de zuòr.** 我想预订中间的座儿。
Could I reserve a table in the middle?	**Wǒ xiǎng yùdìng zài zhōngjiān de zhuōzi.** 我想预订在中间的桌子。
Could I reserve back row seats?	**Wǒ xiǎng yùdìng hòumiàn de zuòr.** 我想预订后面的座儿。
Could I reserve a table in the middle?	**Wǒ xiǎng yùdìng zài zhōngjiān de zhuōzi.** 我想预订在中间的桌子。
Are there any seats left for tonight?	**Hái yǒu méiyǒu jīnwǎn de piào?** 还有没有今晚的票？
How much is a ticket?	**Yì zhāng piào duōshǎo qián?** 一张票多少钱？

When can I pick up
the tickets?

Piào shénme shíhou néng qǔ?
票什么时候能取?

I've got a reservation.
My name's···

Wǒ yùdìngle piào. Wǒde míngzi jiào...
我预订了票。我的名字叫···

你想预定哪个表演?
Nǐ xiǎng yùdìng nar?

Which performance would you
like to reserve (tickets for)?

你想坐在哪儿?
Nǐ xiǎng zuò zài nǎr?

Where would you like to sit?

票都卖光了。
Piào dōu mài guāngle.

Everything's sold out.

只有站的位子。
Zhǐyǒu zhàn de wèizi.

It's standing room only.

我们只有楼厅的票了。
Wǒmén zhǐyǒu lóutīng de piàole.

We've only got circle seat tickets
left.

我们只有上层楼厅的票了。
**Wǒmén zhǐyǒu shàngcéng
lóutīngde piàole.**

We've only got upper circle seat
tickets left.

我们只有前排的票了。
Wǒmén zhǐ shèng qiánpáide piàole.

We've only got tickets for the
front row.

我们只有后排的票了。
**Wǒmén zhǐ shèng hòupáide
piàole.**

We've only got tickets for the
back row.

你要几张票?
Nǐ yào jǐzhāng piào?

How many tickets would you like?

你要在…点前来拾取你的票。
**Nǐ yào zài...dián qián lái shíqǔ
nǐde piào.**

You'll have to pick up the tickets
before...o'clock.

请给我看你的票。
Qǐng gěi wǒ kàn nǐde piào.

Tickets, please.

这是你（们）的座儿。
Zhè shì nǐ(mén)de zuòr.

This is your seat.

（对不起），你坐错位子了。
(Duìbuqǐ), nǐ zuòcuò wèizile.

(Sorry) You are in the wrong seat.

12. Sports Activities

12.1 Sporting questions
12.2 By the waterfront
12.3 In the snow

12.1 Sporting questions

Cycling
Qí zìxíngchē
骑自行车

Skiing
Huáxuě
滑雪

Mountain climbing
Páshān
爬山

Shanghai International
  Circuit (to watch the
  China Grand Prix)
Shànghǎi Guójì Sàichēchǎng
上海国际赛车场

The Dunes at Shenzhou
  Peninsula
Shénzhōu Bàndǎo Shāqiū
神州半岛沙丘

Beijing National Stadium
Guójiā Tǐyùchǎng
国家体育场

Martial arts
Wǔshù
武术

Gymnastics
Tǐcāo
体操

Volleyball
Páiqiú
排球

Basketball
Lánqiú
篮球

Swimming
Yóuyǒng
游泳

Hiking
Yuǎnzú
远足

Fishing
Diàoyú
钓鱼

Football
Zúqiú
足球

Table Tennis
Pīngpāng qiú
乒乓球

Badminton
Yǔmáoqiú
羽毛球

Snowboarding
Huáxuěbǎn
滑雪板

Hot springs
Wēnquán
温泉

Golf
Gāo'ěrfūqiú
高尔夫球

Where's the stadium? **Yùndòngchǎng zài nǎli?**
运动场在哪里?

Where's the gymnasium? **Tǐyùguǎn zài nǎli?** 体育馆在哪里?

Can we see a soccer game? **Wǒmen kěyǐ qù kàn zúqiú bǐsài ma?**
我们可以去看足球比赛吗?

Can we see a basketball game?	**Wǒmen kěyǐ qù kàn lánqiú bǐsài ma?** 我们可以去看篮球比赛吗？
Can we see a badminton game?	**Wǒmen kěyǐ qù kàn yǔmáoqiú bǐsài ma?** 我们可以去看羽毛球比赛吗？
Can we see a table tennis game?	**Wǒmen kěyǐ qù kàn pīngpāng qiú bǐsài ma?** 我们可以去看乒乓球比赛吗？
When does the game begin?	**Bǐsài shénme shíhou kāishǐ?** 比赛什么时候开始？
What's the score?	**Bǐfēn shì duōshao?** 比分是多少？
I've won.	**Wǒ yíng le.** 我赢了。
I've lost.	**Wǒ shū le.** 我输了。
We're even.	**Dǎchéng píngshǒu.** 打成平手。

12.2 By the waterfront

Is it far (to walk) to the sea?	**Zhèlǐ qù hǎibiān yuǎn ma?** 这里去海边远吗？
Is there a swimming pool around here?	**Zhèlǐ yǒu méiyǒu yóuyǒngchí?** 这里有没有游泳池？
Is there a sandy beach around here?	**Zhèlǐ yǒu méiyǒu hǎitān?** 这里有没有海滩？
Are there any rocks here?	**Zhèlǐ yǒu méiyǒu shítou?** 这里有没有石头？
When's high tide?	**Shénme shíhou zhǎng cháo?** 什么时候涨潮？
When's low tide?	**Shénme shíhou tuì cháo?** 什么时候退潮？
What's the water temperature?	**Shuǐwēn shì duōshao?** 水温是多少？

Is it deep here?	**Shuǐ shēn bu shēn?** 水深不深？
Is it safe for children to swim here?	**Xiǎohái zài zhèlǐ yóuyǒng ānquán ma?** 小孩在这里游泳安全吗？
Are there any currents?	**Zhèlǐ yǒu méiyǒu jíliú?** 这里有没有急流？
Are there any sharks?	**Zhèlǐ yǒu méiyǒu shāyú?** 这里有没有鲨鱼？
Are there any jellyfish?	**Zhèlǐ yǒu méiyǒu shuǐmǔ?** 这里有没有水母？
What does that flag mean?	**Nà miàn qí shì shénme yìsi?** 那面旗是什么意思？
What does that buoy mean?	**Nà fúbiāo shì shénme yìsi?** 那浮标是什么意思？
Is there a lifeguard on duty?	**Zhèlǐ yǒu méiyǒu jiùshēngyuán zhíbān?** 这里有没有救生员值班？
Where can I get a chair?	**Nǎli yǒu yǐzi?** 哪里有椅子？
Where can I get a beach umbrella?	**Nǎli yǒu tàiyáng sǎn?** 哪里有太阳伞？
Where can I get a towel?	**Nǎli yǒu máojīn?** 哪里有毛巾？
Where can I get sunglasses?	**Nǎli yǒu mòjìng?** 哪里有墨镜？
Where can I get sunscreen?	**Nǎli yǒu fángshài shuāng?** 哪里有防晒霜？
Where can I have a shower?	**Nǎli kěyǐ línyù?** 哪里可以淋浴？

Danger **Wēixiǎn** 危险	No swimming/fishing here. **Zhèlǐ bùzhǔn yóuyǒng/diàoyú.** 这里不准游泳／钓鱼。

12.3 In the snow

Can I take snowboarding lessons here?	**Zhèlǐ yǒu méiyǒu xué huáxuěbǎn de bān?** 这里有没有学滑雪板的班?
Can I take skiing lessons here?	**Zhèlǐ yǒu méiyǒu xué huáxuě de bān?** 这里有没有学滑雪的班?
Can I rent the gear from here?	**Zhèlǐ kěyi zū huáxuě zhuāng bèi ma?** 这里可以租滑雪装备吗?
For beginners	**Chūjíbān** 初级班
For intermediates	**Zhōngjíbān** 中级班
How large are the classes?	**Yìbān yǒu duōshao rén?** 一班有多少人?
What languages are the classes in?	**Shàngkè jiǎng shénme yǔyán?** 上课讲什么语言?
I'd like a lift pass, please.	**Qǐng gěi wǒ diàolánpiào.** 请给我吊篮票。
Where are the beginners' slopes?	**Chūjí huáxuědào zài nǎli?** 初级滑雪道在哪里?
Where are the intermediate runs?	**Zhōngjí huáxuědào zài nǎli?** 中级滑雪道在哪里?
Are there any cross-country ski runs around here?	**Zhèlǐ yǒu méiyǒu yuèyě huáxuědào?** 这里有没有越野滑雪道?
Have the cross-country runs been marked?	**Yuèyě huáxuědào yǒu méiyǒu biāozhì?** 越野滑雪道有没有标志?
Are the ski lifts open?	**Huáxuě diàolán kāi bu kāi?** 滑雪吊篮开不开?

Are the chair lifts open? **Shàngshān diàochē kāi bu kāi?**
上山吊车开不开?

Are the runs open? **Huáxuědào kāi bu kāi?**
滑雪道开不开?

Are the cross-country
 runs open? **Yuèyě huáxuědào kāi bu kāi?**
越野滑雪道开不开?

13. Health Matters

13.1 Calling a doctor
13.2 What's wrong?
13.3 The consultation
13.4 Medications and prescriptions
13.5 At the dentist

If you get sick or need emergency treatment, you can call 120 or 999. There are special departments for foreign nationals in many large hospitals where they have better facilities, although it will be more expensive. Otherwise, go to the Casualty department at the nearest hospital. You should register first, have your illness treated and then settle the bill.

13.1 Calling a doctor

Could you call (get) a doctor quickly, please?	**Qǐng gěi wǒ zhǎo ge yīshēng.** 请给我找个医生。
When are the doctor's working hours?	**Yīshēng jǐdiǎn dào jǐdiǎn kànbìng?** 医生几点到几点看病？
When can the doctor come?	**Yīshēng shénme shíhou néng lái?** 医生什么时候能来？
Could I make an appointment to see the doctor?	**Wǒ xiǎng yùyuē kànbìng, kěyǐ ma?** 我想预约看病，可以吗？
I've got an appointment to see the doctor at four o'clock.	**Wǒ gēn yīshēng yùyuēhǎo sìdiǎnzhōng kànbìng.** 我跟预约好四点钟看病。
Which pharmacy is on night duty?	**Nǎ ge yàofáng wǎnshang yíngyè?** 哪个药房晚上营业？
Which pharmacy is on weekend duty?	**Nǎ ge yàofáng zhōumò yíngyè?** 哪个药房周末营业？

13.2 What's wrong?

I don't feel well.	**Wǒ bú tài shūfu.** 我不太舒服。
I'm ill.	**Wǒ bìng le.** 我病了。
I'm dizzy.	**Wǒ tóuyūn.** 我头晕。
I feel sick (nauseous).	**Wǒ xiǎng tù.** 我想吐。
I've got a cold.	**Wǒ gǎnmào le.** 我感冒了。
I've got a cough.	**Wǒ késou.** 我咳嗽。
I've got diarrhea.	**Wǒ fùxiè/lā dùzi le.** 我腹泻/拉肚子了。
I have trouble breathing.	**Wǒ gǎnjué hūxī kùnnan.** 我感觉呼吸困难。
I feel tired all over.	**Wǒ húnshēn méijìn.** 我浑身没劲。
It hurts here.	**Zhèlǐ téng.** 这里疼。
I've been sick (vomited).	**Wǒ ǒutù le.** 我呕吐了。
I'm running a temperature of…degrees	**Wǒ fāshāo, ...dù** 我发烧，…度
I've been stung by a wasp.	**Wǒ bèi huángfēng zhēle.** 我被黄蜂蛰了。
I've been stung by an insect.	**Wǒ bèi shénme chóngzi zhēle.** 我被什么虫子蛰了。
I've been stung by a jellyfish.	**Wǒ bèi shuǐmǔ zhēle.** 我被水母蛰了。
I've been bitten by a dog.	**Wǒ bèi gǒu yǎole.** 我被狗咬了。
I've been bitten by a snake.	**Wǒ bèi shé yǎole.** 我被蛇咬了。
I've cut myself.	**Wǒ gēshāng zìjǐ le.** 我割伤自己了。
I've burned myself.	**Wǒ shāoshāng zìjǐ le.** 我烧伤自己了。

I've grazed myself.	**Wǒ cāshāng zìjǐ le.** 我擦伤自己了。
I've scratched myself.	**Wǒ zhuāshāng zìjǐ le.** 我抓伤自己了。
I've had a fall.	**Wǒ diēshāng le.** 我跌伤了。

13.3 The consultation

你哪里不舒服？
Nǐ nǎlǐ bù shūfu?

What seems to be the problem?

你有这个病情多久了？
Nǐ yǒu zhège bìngqíng duōjiǔle?

How long have you had these complaints?

以前有过这个病吗？
Yǐqián yǒuguò zhè ge bìng ma?

Have you had this trouble before?

发烧吗？多少度？
Fāshāo ma? Duōshao dù?

Do you have a temperature? How high is it?

请解开上衣。
Qǐng jiěkāi shàngyī.

Open your shirt, please.

请脱下上衣。
Qǐng tuōxià shàngyī.

Strip to the waist, please.

你可以在这里脱衣服。
Nǐ kěyǐ zài zhèlǐ tuō yīfu.

You can undress here.

请卷起左袖子。
Qǐng juǎn qǐ zuǒ xiùzi.

Roll up your left sleeve, please.

请卷起右袖子。
Qǐng juǎn qǐ yòu xiùzi.

Roll up your right sleeve, please.

请躺在这里。
Qǐng tǎng zài zhèlǐ.

Lie down here, please.

疼不疼？
Téng bù téng?

Does this hurt?

深呼吸。
Shēnhūxī.

Breathe deeply.

张开嘴。
Zhāngkāi zuǐ.

Open your mouth.

I've sprained my ankle.	**Wǒ niǔshāng le wǒde jiǎohuái.** 我扭伤了我的脚踝。

Could I have a female doctor, please?	**Qǐng gěi wǒ zhǎo yí wèi nǚ yīshēng.** 请给我找一位女医生。
I'd like the morning-after pill.	**Wǒ yàomǎi shìhòu bìyùnyào.** 我要买事后避孕药。

Patients' medical history

I'm a diabetic.	**Wǒ yǒu tángniàobìng.** 我有糖尿病。
I'm asthmatic.	**Wǒ yǒu xiàochuǎn.** 我有哮喘。
I'm allergic to penicillin.	**Wǒ duì qīngméisù guòmǐn de.** 我对青霉素过敏的。
I'm allergic to amoxillin.	**Wǒ duì āmòxīlín guòmǐn de.** 我对阿莫西林过敏的。
I have a heart condition.	**Wǒ yǒu xīnzàngbìng.** 我有心脏病。
I'm five months pregnant.	**Wǒ huáiyùn wǔge yuè.** 我怀孕五个月。
I'm on a diet.	**Wǒ zài jiéshí.** 我在节食。
I'm on medication.	**Wǒ zài fú yàowù.** 我在服药物。
I'm on the pill.	**Wǒ zài fú bìyùnyào.** 我在服避孕药。
I've had a heart attack. once before.	**Wǒ céng yǒuguò yí cì xīnzàngbìng fāzuò.** 我曾有过一次心脏病发作。

你对什么过敏? **Nǐ duì shénme guòmǐn?**	Do you have any allergies?
你现在吃什么药? **Nǐ xiànzài chī shénme yào?**	Are you on any medication?
你是不是在节食? **Nǐ shì bushì zài jiéshí?**	Are you on a diet?
你怀孕了吗? **Nǐ huáiyùnle ma?**	Are you pregnant?
你打过破伤风针吗? **Nǐ dǎguò pòshāngfēng zhēn ma?**	Have you had a tetanus injection?

I've had a(n)…operation.   **Wǒ yǐqián zuòguò...shǒushù.**
我以前做过…手术。

I've been ill recently.   **Wǒ zuìjìn bìngguo yí cì.**
我最近病过一次。

The diagnosis

不要紧。   It's nothing serious.
Búyàojǐn

你的…断了。   Your…is broken.
Nǐ de...duàn le.

你扭伤了。   You've got a sprained…
Nǐ niǔshāng le.

你的…扯破了。   You've got a torn…
Nǐ de...chěpò le.

你感染／发炎了。   You've got an infection.
Nǐ gǎnrǎn/fāyán le.

你的…发炎了。   You've got some inflammation.
Nǐ de...fāyán le.

你得了阑尾炎。   You've got appendicitis.
Nǐ dé le lánwěiyán.

你得了气管炎。   You've got bronchitis.
Nǐ dé le qìguǎnyán.

你得了性病。   You've got a venereal disease.
Nǐ dé le xìngbìng.

你得了感冒。   You've got the flu.
Nǐ dé le gǎnmào.

你的心脏病发作了。   You've had a heart attack.
Nǐ de xīnzàngbìng fāzuò le.

你得了肺炎。   You've got pneumonia.
Nǐ dé le fèiyán.

你得了胃炎。   You've got gastritis.
Nǐ dé le wèiyán.

你得了胃溃疡。   You've got an ulcer.
Nǐ dé le wèikuìyáng.

你扯伤了肌肉。   You've pulled a muscle.
Nǐ chěshāng le jīròu.

你的阴道发炎了。   You've got a vaginal infection.
Nǐde yīndào fāyán le.

你食物中毒了。
Nǐ shíwù zhòngdú le.

You've got food poisoning.

你中暑了。
Nǐ zhòngshǔ le.

You've got sunstroke.

你对…过敏。
Nǐ duì...guòmǐn.

You're allergic to…

你怀孕了。
Nǐ huáiyùn le.

You're pregnant.

我要给你化验你的血。
Wǒ yào gěi nǐ huàyàn nǐde xiě.

I'd like to have your blood tested.

我要给你化验你的尿。
Wǒ yào gěi nǐ huàyàn nǐde niào.

I'd like to have your urine tested.

我要给你化验你的大便。
Wǒ yào gěi nǐ huàyàn nǐde dàbiàn.

I'd like to have your stools tested.

要缝合伤口。
Yào fénghé shāngkǒu.

It needs stitches.

我把你交给专科医生。
Wǒ bǎ nǐ jiāo gěi zhuānkē yīshēng.

I'm referring you to a specialist.

我把你送进医院。
Wǒ bǎ nǐ sòng jìn yīyuàn.

I'm sending you to the hospital.

你要去做透视。
Nǐ yào qù zuò tòushì.

You'll need some x-rays taken.

请你在候诊室等候。
Qǐng nǐ zài hòuzhěnshì děnghòu.

Could you wait in the waiting room, please?

你需要做手术。
Nǐ xūyào zuò shǒushù.

You'll need an operation.

I need something for diarrhea.

Wǒ yào zhì fùxiè de yào.
我要治腹泻的药。

I need something for a cold.

Wǒ yào zhì gǎnmào de yào.
我要治感冒的药。

I've got a stomach ulcer.

Wǒ yǒu wèikuìyáng. 我有胃溃疡。

I've got my period.

Wǒ yuèjīng gāng lái. 我月经刚来。

Is it contagious?

Huì chuánrǎn ma? 会传染吗？

How long do I have to stay in bed?

Wǒ yào tǎng zài chuángshàng duōjiǔ?
我要躺在床上多久？

How long do I have to stay in the hospital?	**Wǒ yào zhùyuàn duōjiǔ?** 我要住院多久?
Do I have to go on a special diet?	**Wǒ yào tèbié jiéshí ma?** 我要特别节食吗?
Am I allowed to travel?	**Wǒ kěyǐ qù lǚyóu ma?** 我可以去旅游吗?
Can I make another appointment?	**Wǒ kěyǐ zài yùyuē ge shíjiān ma?** 我可以再预约个时间吗?
How do I take this medicine?	**Zhè zhǒng yào zěnme chī?** 这种药怎么吃?

13.4 Medications and prescriptions

How many pills each time?	**Měi cì duōshao piàn?** 每次多少片?
How many drops each time?	**Měi cì duōshao dī?** 每次多少滴?
How many spoonfuls each time?	**Měi cì duōshao sháo?** 每次多少勺?
How many tablets each time?	**Měi cì duōshao lì?** 每次多少粒?
How many injections each time?	**Měi cì dǎ jǐ zhēn?** 每次打几针?
How many times a day?	**Yì tiān duōshao cì?** 一天多少次?
I've forgotten my medication.	**Wǒ wàngle chī yào.** 我忘了吃药。
At home I take...	**Zài jiā wǒ chī...** 在家我吃…
Could you write a prescription for me, please?	**Qǐng gěi wǒ kāi ge yàofāng.** 请给我开个药方。

我给你开抗生素。
Wǒ gěi nǐ kāi kàngshēngsù.

I'm prescribing antibiotics.

我给你开咳嗽药水。
Wǒ gěi nǐ kāi késou yàoshuǐ.

I'm prescribing a cough mixture.

我给你开镇静剂。
Wǒ gěi nǐ kāi zhènjìngjì.

I'm prescribing a tranquilizer.

我给你开止痛药。
Wǒ gěi nǐ kāi zhǐtòng yào.

I'm prescribing painkillers.

好好休息。
Hǎohǎo xiūxí.

Have lots of rest.

不要外出。
Búyào wàichū.

Stay indoors.

躺在床上。
Tǎng zài chuángshàng.

Stay in bed.

请明天回来复诊。
Qǐng míngtiān huílái fùzhěn.

Come back tomorrow.

请三天后回来复诊。
Qǐng sān tiān hòu huílái fùzhěn.

Come back in three days' time.

Rub on
Róucuo
揉搓

Spoonful
Sháo
勺

Swallow
Tūn xià
吞下

Before meals
Fàn qián
饭前

Teaspoonful
Cháshao
茶勺

External use only
Wàiyòng
外用

After meals
Fàn hòu
饭后

Finish the prescription.
Quánbù chī wán yīshēng kāi de yào.
全部吃完医生开的药。

Dissolve in water
Rónghuà zài shuǐlǐ
溶化在水里

For…days
…Tiān
…天

Every…hours
Měi…zhōngtóu
每…钟头

…times a day
Měi tiān…cì
每天…次

Injections
Dǎzhēn
打针

This medication impairs your driving.
Zhè zhǒng yào yǐngxiǎng kāichē.
这种药影响开车。

Take (eat)
Chī
吃

Ointment
Yàogāo
药膏

Take (drink)
Hē
喝

13.5 At the dentist

Do you know a good
dentist?

Zhèlǐ yǒu hǎo de yákē yīshēng ma?
这里有好的牙科医生吗?

Could you make a dentist's
appointment for me?

Qǐng gěi wǒ yùyuē yákē yīshēng.
请给我预约牙科医生。

It's urgent.

Zhè shì jǐnjí de. 这是紧急的。

Can I come in today,
please?

Wǒ néng jīntiān lái ma?
我能今天来吗?

I have a (terrible)
toothache.

Wǒde yá téngsǐ wǒ le.
我的牙疼死我了。

Could you prescribe/
give me a painkiller?

Kěyǐ gěi wǒ kāi ge zhǐtòngyào ma?
可以给我开个止痛药吗?

I've got a broken tooth.

Wǒde yá zhuànghuàile. 我的牙撞坏了。

I've got a broken crown.

Wǒde chǐguān zhuànghuàile.
我的齿冠撞坏了。

I've got a broken denture.

Wǒde jiǎyá zhuànghuàile.
我的假牙撞坏了。

My filling's come out.

Wǒ bǔyáde tiánchōngwù diàochūlai le.
我补牙的填充物掉出来了。

I'd like a local anaesthetic.

Qǐng gěi wǒ dǎ máyào.
请给我打麻药。

I don't want a
local anaesthetic.

Qǐng búyào gěi wǒ dǎ máyào.
请不要给我打麻药。

I'm giving you a local
anaesthetic.

Wǒ xiànzài gěi nǐ dǎ máyào.
我现在给你打麻药。

Could you do a
temporary repair?

Kěyǐ gěi wǒ línshí bǔ yì bǔ yá ma?
可以给我临时补一补牙吗?

I don't want this tooth
pulled.

Wǒ búyào bá zhè kē yá.
我不要拔这颗牙。

14. Emergencies

14.1 Asking for help

Help!	**Jiùmìng a!** 救命啊!
Get help quickly!	**Kuài jiào rén lái bāngmáng!** 快叫人来帮忙!
Fire!	**Jiùhuǒ la!** 救火啦!
Police!	**Wǒ yào jǐngchá!** 我要警察!
Get a doctor!	**Qù zhǎo yīshēng lái!** 去找医生来!
Quick/Hurry!	**Kuài!** 快!
Watch out!	**Dāngxīn!** 当心!
Be careful!	**Xiǎoxīn!** 小心!
Danger!	**Wēixiǎn!** 危险!
Stop!	**Tíngzhù!** 停住!
Get your hands off me!	**Nákāi nǐde shǒu!** 拿开你的手!
Let go!	**Fàngkāi wǒ!** 放开我!
Stop thief!	**Zhuā zéi la!** 抓贼啦!
Could you help me, please?	**Qǐng bāng ge máng, kěyǐ ma?** 请帮个忙,可以吗?
Where's the police station?	**Gōng'ānjú (Jǐngchájú) zài nǎli?** 公安局(警察局)在哪里?
Where's the emergency exit?	**Jǐnjí chūkǒu zài nǎli?** 紧急出口在哪里?

Where's the fire escape?	**Tàipíngtī zài nǎli?** 太平梯在哪里？
Call the fire department!	**Kuài jiào xiāofángjú!** 快叫消防局！
Call the police!	**Kuài jiào jǐngchá!** 快叫警察！
Call the ambulance!	**Kuài jiào jiùhùchē!** 快叫救护车！
Where's the nearest phone?	**Zuìjìnde diànhuà zài nǎlǐ?** 最近的电话在哪里？
Could I use your phone?	**Kěyǐ jièyòng nǐde diànhuà ma?** 可以借用你的电话吗？
What's the emergency number?	**Jǐnjí hàomǎ shì shénme?** 紧急号码是什么？
What's the number for the police?	**Gōng'ānjú/jǐngchájú de diànhuà shì shénme?** 公安局／警察局的电话是什么？

14.2 Lost items

I've lost my wallet.	**Wǒ diūshīle qiánbāo.** 我丢失了钱包。
I've lost my laptop.	**Wǒ diūshīle bǐjìběn diànnǎo.** 我丢失了笔记本电脑。
I've lost my passport.	**Wǒ diūshīle hùzhào.** 我丢失了护照。
I've lost my mobile phone.	**Wǒ diūshīle shǒujī.** 我丢失了手机。
I lost my mobile phone here yesterday.	**Wǒ zuótiān zài zhèlǐ diūle wǒde shǒujī.** 我昨天在这里丢了我的手机。
I left my wallet here.	**Wǒ zài zhèlǐ diūxià wǒde qiánbāo.** 我在这里丢下我的钱包。
Did you find my wallet?	**Nǐ zhǎodào wǒde qiánbāo le ma?** 你找到我的钱包了吗？
It was right here.	**Wǒ jìde shì fàng zài zhèlǐ de.** 我记得是放在这里的。
It's very valuable.	**Zhè shì hěn guìzhòng de.** 这是很贵重的。
Where's the lost and found office?	**Shīwù zhāolǐngchù zài nǎli?** 失物招领处在哪里？

14.3 Accidents

There's been an accident.
(Wǒmen) zhèr chū shìgù le.
(我们)这儿出事故了。

Someone's fallen into the water.
Yǒurén diàojìn shuǐlǐ le!
有人掉进水里了!

There's a fire.
Zháohuǒ le! 着火了!

Is anyone hurt?
Yǒu méiyǒu rén shòushāng?
有没有人受伤?

Nobody has been injured.
Méi rén shòushāng le. 没人受伤了。

Someone has been injured.
Yǒu rén shòushāng le. 有人受伤了。

Someone's still trapped inside the car.
Yǒu rén hái kùn zài chē lǐmiàn.
有人还困在车里面。

It's not too bad.
Hál suàn hǎo. 还算好。

Don't worry.
Búyào dānxīn. 不要担心。

Leave everything the way it is, please.
Qǐng ràng suǒyǒu de dōngxi bǎochí yuánzhuàng.
请让所有的东西保持原状。

I want to talk to the police first.
Wǒ yào xiān gēn jǐngchá tántan.
我要先跟警察谈谈。

I want to take a photo first.
Wǒ yào xiān pāi ge zhào.
我要先拍个照。

Here's my name, mobile number and address.
Zhè shì wǒde míngzì, shǒujī hàomǎ hé dìzhǐ.
这是我的名字,手机号码和地址。

May I have your name, phone number and address?
Qǐng gěi wǒ nǐde míngzì, shǒujī hàomǎ hé dìzhǐ.
请给我你的名字,手机号码和地址。

Could I see your identity card?
Qǐng gěi wǒ kànkan nǐde shēnfènzhèng.
请给我看看你的身份证。

Could I see your insurance papers?
Qǐng gěi wǒ kànkan nǐde bǎoxiǎndān.
请给我看看你的保险单。

Could I see your passport?	**Qǐng gěi wǒ kànkan nǐde hùzhào.** 请给我看看你的护照。
Will you act as a witness?	**Nǐ yuànyì zuò zhèng ma?** 你愿意作证吗？
I need this information for insurance purposes.	**Wǒde bǎoxiǎn gōngsī xūyào zhèxiē zīliào.** 我的保险公司需要这些资料。
Are you insured?	**Nǐ yǒu bǎoxiǎn ma?** 你有保险吗？
Third party or all inclusive?	**Nǐ mǎi de bǎoxiǎn shì dìsānzhě bǎoxiǎn háishì quánbǎo?** 你买的保险是第三者保险还是全保？
Could you sign here, please?	**Qǐng zài zhèlǐ qiān ge míng.** 请在这里签个名。

14.4 Theft

I've been robbed.	**Wǒ bèi qiǎngjié le.** 我被抢劫了。
My mobile phone has been stolen.	**Wǒde shǒujī bèi rén tōu le.** 我的手机被人偷了。
My car's been broken into.	**Wǒde qìchē bèi zéi qiàokāi le.** 我的汽车被贼撬开了。

14.5 Missing person

I've lost my child.	**Wǒ de háizi diūshīle.** 我的孩子丢失了。
Could you help me find him?	**Nǐ néng bāng wǒ zhǎo tā ma?** 你能帮我找他吗？
Could you help me find her?	**Nǐ néng bāng wǒ zhǎo tā ma?** 你能帮我找她吗？
He's five years old.	**Tā wǔsuì.** 他五岁。
She's nine years old.	**Tā jiǔ suì.** 她九岁。
He's got short blond hair.	**Tā yǒu duǎn jīnfa.** 他有短金发。
She's got long red hair.	**Tā yǒu cháng hóngfa.** 她有长红发。

He's got curly brown hair.	**Tā yǒu zōngsède juǎnfà.** 他有棕色的卷发。
She's got straight black hair.	**Tā yǒu hēisède zhífà.** 她有黑色的直发。
He's got frizzy hair.	**Tā yǒu xiǎojuǎnjié.** 他有小卷结。
She's wearing a ponytail.	**Tāde tóufa shì shū mǎwěi de.** 她的头发是梳马尾的。
She's wearing braids.	**Tāde tóufa shì shū biànzi de.** 她的头发是梳辫子的。
She's wearing her hair in a bun.	**Tāde tóufa shì shū fàjì de.** 她的头发是梳发髻的。
He's got blue eyes.	**Tāde yǎnjing shì lánsè de.** 他的眼睛是蓝色的。
She's got brown eyes.	**Tāde yǎnjing shì zōngsè de.** 她的眼睛是棕色的。
He's got green eyes.	**Tāde yǎnjing shì lǜsè de.** 他的眼睛是绿色的。
He's wearing a red shirt and jeans.	**Tā chuānzhe hóngsède chènshān hé nǐuzǎikù.** 他穿着红色的衬衫和牛仔裤。
She's wearing a blue blouse and black pants.	**Tā chuānzhe lánsède nǚ chènshān hé hēikùzi.** 她穿着蓝色的女衬衫和黑裤子。
He's wearing glasses.	**Tā dàizhe yǎnjìng.** 他戴着眼镜。
She's not wearing glasses.	**Tā méi dàizhe yǎnjìng.** 她没戴着眼镜。
He's carrying a bag.	**Tā shǒu názhe yí ge dàizi.** 他手拿着一个袋子。
She's not carrying a bag.	**Tā méi názhe yí ge dàizi.** 她没拿着一个袋子。
He is tall.	**Tā zhǎngde gāo.** 他长得高。
She is short.	**Tā zhǎngde ǎi.** 她长得矮。
This is a photo of him/her.	**Zhè shì tāde zhàopiàn.** 这是他／她的照片。

14.6 The police

An arrest

I don't speak Chinese.	**Wǒ búhuì shuō Hànyǔ/Zhōngwén.** 我不会说汉语／中文。
I didn't see the sign.	**Wǒ méi kànjiàn biāozhì.** 我没看见标志。
I don't understand what it says.	**Wǒ kànbudǒng shàngmiàn shuō shénme.** 我看不懂上面说什么。
I was only doing... kilometers an hour.	**Wǒde sùdù měi xiǎoshí zhǐ shì...gōnglǐ.** 我的速度每小时只是…公里。
I'll have my car checked.	**Wǒ mǎshàng qù xiūlǐ qìchē.** 我马上去修理汽车。
I was blinded by oncoming lights.	**Kāiguòlái de chēdēng zhào de wǒ yǎnjīng hūnhā.** 开过来的车灯照得我眼睛昏花。

请给我你的驾驶证。 **Qǐng gěi wǒ nǐde jiàshǐzhèng.**	Your (vehicle) documents, please.
你超速了。 **Nǐ chāosùle.**	You were speeding.
这里不能停放车辆。 **Zhèlǐ bùnéng tíngfàng chēliàng.**	You're not allowed to park here.
你没有在计时器里投钱。 **Nǐ méiyǒu zài jìshíqì lǐ tóuqián.**	You haven't put money in the parking meter.
你的前灯不亮。 **Nǐ de qiándēng bú liàng.**	Your front lights aren't working.
你的后灯不亮。 **Nǐ de hòudēng bú liàng.**	Your rear lights aren't working.
这是…罚款。 **Zhè shì …fákuǎn.**	That's a ...fine.
你想现在付款吗? **Nǐ xiǎng xiànzài fùkuǎn ma?**	Do you want to pay now?
你得现在付款。 **Nǐ děi xiànzài fùkuǎn.**	You'll have to pay now.

At the police station

I want to report a collision.	**Wǒ yào bào zhuàngchē de ànzi.** 我要报撞车的案子。
I want to file a report for a missing person.	**Wǒ yào bào shīzōng de ànzi.** 我要报失踪的案子。
Could you make a statement, please?	**Nǐ néng zuò bǐgòng ma?** 你能作笔供吗？
Could I have a copy for the insurance?	**Wǒ néng yào yí fèn bǎoxiǎndān de fùběn ma?** 我能要一份保险单的副本吗？
I've no money left, I'm desperate.	**Wǒde qián yě diū le, wǒ zǒutóu wúlù le.** 我的钱也丢了，我走投无路了。
I'd like an interpreter.	**Wǒ xūyào fānyì.** 我需要翻译。
I'm innocent.	**Wǒ shì wúgū de.** 我是无辜的。
I want to speak to someone from the American Embassy.	**Wǒ yào gēn Měiguó Dàshǐguǎn de rén shuōhuà.** 我要跟美国大使馆的人说话。
I want a lawyer who speaks English.	**Wǒ yào zhǎo huì shuō Yīngyǔde lǜshī.** 我要找会说英语的律师。

Emergencies

14

在哪里发生的？ **Zài nǎlǐ fāshēng de?**	Where did it happen?
什么时候发生的？ **Shénme shíhou fāshēng de?**	What time did it happen?
你丢失了什么？ **Nǐ diūshīle shénme?**	What's missing?
小偷拿了什么？ **Xiǎotōu nále shénme?**	What's been taken?
有没有证人？ **Yǒu méiyǒu zhèngrén?**	Are there any witnesses?
你需要翻译吗？ **Nǐ xūyào fānyì ma?**	Do you want an interpreter?

15. English-Chinese Dictionary

The following dictionary is meant to supplement the chapters in this book. Some of the words not on this list can be found elsewhere in this book. Food items can be found in sections 4.7 and 4.8, and the parts of a car on page 77 and the parts of a bicycle on page 83.

A

abacus **suànpán** 算盘

about (approximately) **dàyuē** 大约

above **shàngmiàn** 上面

abroad **guówài** 国外

accident **shìgù** 事故

acrobatics troupe **zájìtuán** 杂技团

adapt (verb) **shìyìng** 适应

adaptor **chāzuò** 插座

address **dìzhǐ** 地址

admission **rùchǎng** 入场

admission price **rùchǎngfèi/ménpiàofèi** 入场费／门票费

adult **chéngrén** 成人

advice **jiànyì** 建议

after **zài...yǐhòu** 在…以后

afternoon **xiàwǔ** 下午

aftershave **xūhòushuǐ** 须后水

again **zài** 再

against **fǎnduì** 反对

age **niánlíng** 年龄

agree **tóngyì** 同意

AIDS **àizībìng** 艾滋病

air **kōngqì** 空气

air conditioning **kōngtiáo** 空调

air mattress **qìdiàn** 气垫

air pollution **kōngqì wūrǎn** 空气污染

airmail **hángkōng yóujiàn** 航空邮件

airplane **fēijī** 飞机

airport **fēijīchǎng** 飞机场

alarm **jǐngzhōng** 警钟

alarm clock **nàozhōng** 闹钟

alcohol **jiǔ** 酒

all day **quántiān** 全天

all the time **zǒngshì** 总是

allergy **guòmǐn** 过敏

alone **dāndú** 单独

also **yě** 也

altogether **yígòng** 一共

always **zǒngshì** 总是

ambulance **jiùhùchē** 救护车

America **Měiguó** 美国

American (in general) **Měiguó de** 美国的

American (people) **Měiguórén** 美国人

amount **shùliàng** 数量

amusement park **yóulèchǎng** 游乐场

anaesthetic (general) **quánshēn mázuì** 全身麻醉

anaesthetic (local) **júbù mázuì** 局部麻醉

angry **shēngqì** 生气

animal **dòngwù** 动物

ankle **huái** 踝

answer **huídá** 回答

ant **mǎyǐ** 蚂蚁

antibiotics **kàngshēngsù** 抗生素

antique **gǔjiù** 古旧

antiques **gǔwán** 古玩

antiseptic **fángfùjì** 防腐剂

anus **gāngmén** 肛门

any **rènhé** 任何

anyone **rènhé rén** 任何人

apartment **gōngyù** 公寓

apologies **dàoqiàn** 道歉

apple **píngguǒ** 苹果

apple juice **píngguǒzhī** 苹果汁

appointment (meeting) **yùyuē** 预约

April **Sìyuè** 四月

architecture **jiànzhù** 建筑

area **dìqū** 地区

area code **qūhào** 区号

argue **zhēngchǎo** 争吵

arm **gēbo** 胳膊

arrange **chóubàn/ānpái** 筹办／安排

arrive **dào** 到

art **yìshù** 艺术

artery **xuèguǎn/dòngmài** 血管／动脉

artificial respiration **réngōng hūxī** 人工呼吸

arts and crafts **gōngyì měishù** 工艺美术

ashtray **yānhuīgāng** 烟灰缸

ask (verb) **wèn** 问

ask for **yào** 要

aspirin **āsīpǐlín** 阿司匹林

asthma **xiàochuǎn** 哮喘

at **zài** 在

at home **zài jiā** 在家

at night **wǎnshang** 晚上

at the back **hòumiàn** 后面

at the front **qiánmiàn** 前面

at the latest **zuìchí/zuìwǎn** 最迟／最晚

August **Bāyuè** 八月

Australia **Àodàlìyà/Àozhōu** 澳大利亚／澳洲

Australian (in general) **Àodàlìyàde/Àozhōude** 澳大利亚的／澳洲的

Australian (people) **Àodàlìyàrén/Àozhōurén** 澳大利亚人／澳洲人

automatic **zìdòngde** 自动的

autumn **qiūtiān** 秋天

avoid **bìmiǎn** 避免

awake **xǐng** 醒

B

baby **yīng'ér** 婴儿

baby food **yīng'ér shípǐn** 婴儿食品

babysitter **línshí bǎomǔ** 临时保姆

back (part of body) **bèi** 背

back (rear) **hòumiàn** 后面

backpack **bēibāo** 背包

backpacker **bēibāo-lǚxíngzhě** 背包旅行者

bad (rotting) **chòu** 臭

bad (terrible) **huài/zāo** 坏／糟

bag **dàizi** 袋子

baggage **xíngli** 行李

ball **qiú** 球

ballpoint pen **yuánzhūbǐ** 圆珠笔

banana **xiāngjiāo** 香蕉

Band Aid **chuàngkětiē** 创可贴

bandage **bēngdài** 绷带

bank (finance) **yínháng** 银行

bank (river) **hé'àn** 河岸

banquet **yànhuì** 宴会

bar (cafè) **jiǔbā** 酒吧

barbecue **shāokǎo** 烧烤

barber **lǐ fàdiàn** 理发店

bargain **jiǎngjià** 讲价

baseball **bàngqiú** 棒球

basketball **lánqiú** 篮球

bath towel **yùjīn** 浴巾

bathe **xǐzǎo** 洗澡

bathmat **yùshì fánghuádiàn** 浴室防滑垫

bathrobe **yùyī** 浴衣

bathroom (bathing) **yùshì** 浴室

bathroom (lavatory) **xǐshǒujiān/cèsuǒ** 洗手间／厕所

bathtub **yùgāng/yùpén** 浴缸／浴盆

battery **diànchí** 电池

beach **hǎitān** 海滩

beancurd **dòufu** 豆腐

beautiful **piàoliang/měilì** 漂亮／美丽

beauty parlor **měiróngyuàn** 美容院

because **yīnwèi** 因为

bed **chuáng** 床

bedding **bèirù** 被褥

bedroom **wòshì** 卧室

beef **niúròu** 牛肉

beer **píjiǔ** 啤酒

before **yǐqián** 以前

beggar **qǐgài** 乞丐

begin **kāishǐ** 开始

behind **zài...hòumiàn** 在···后面

Beijing opera **Jīngjù** 京剧

below **zài...xiàmiàn** 在···下面

belt **yāodài** 腰带

berth **wòpù** 卧铺

beside **zài...pángbiān** 在···旁边

best **zuì hǎo** 最好

better **bǐjiào hǎo** 比较好

better (to get) **hǎozhuǎn** 好转

between **zài...zhījiān** 在···之间

bicycle **zìxíngchē** 自行车

big **dà** 大

bikini **sāndiǎnshì yǒngyī/bǐjīní** 三点式泳衣／比基尼

bill **zhàngdān** 帐单

billiards **zhuōqiú** 桌球

bird **niǎo** 鸟

birthday **shēngrì** 生日

biscuit **bǐnggān** 饼干

bite **yǎo** 咬

bitter **kǔde** 苦的

black **hēisè** 黑色

black and white **hēibái** 黑白

black eye **hēiyǎnquān** 黑眼圈

bland (taste) **dāndiāo** 单调

blanket **tǎnzi** 毯子

bleach (verb) **piàobái** 漂白

bleed **liúxuè** 流血

blind (can't see) **kànbujiàn** 看不见

blind (on window) **chuānglián** 窗帘

blister **shuǐpào** 水疱

blog **bókè** 博客

blond **jīnfà** 金发

blood **xuè** 血

blood pressure **xuèyā** 血压

blood transfusion **shūxuè** 输血

blouse **nǚ chènshān** 女衬衫

blue **lánsè** 蓝色

boarding gate **dēngjīmén** 登机门

boat **chuán** 船

body **shēntǐ** 身体

boiled water **kāishuǐ** 开水

bone **gǔtou** 骨头

book **shū** 书

booked, reserved **yùdìngle** 预订了

booking office **dìngpiàochù** 订票处

bookshop **shūdiàn** 书店

border **biānjiè** 边界

bored/boring **mèn/wúliáo** 闷／无聊

born **chūshēng** 出生

borrow **jiè** 借

botanic gardens **zhíwùyuán** 植物园

both **liǎng ge** 两个

bottle (baby's) **nǎipíng** 奶瓶

bottle (wine) **píngzi** 瓶子

bottle-warmer **nuǎnpíngqì** 暖瓶器

bottle opener **kāipíngqì** 开瓶器

bowl **wǎn** 碗

box **hézi** 盒子

box office **piàofáng** 票房

boy **nánháir** 男孩儿

boyfriend **nánpéngyou** 男朋友

bra **rǔzhào** 乳罩

bracelet **shǒuzhuó** 手镯

braised **chǎo** 炒

brake **shāchē** 刹车

brake oil **shāchēyóu** 刹车油

bread **miànbāo** 面包

break (verb) **nònghuài** 弄坏

breakfast **zǎofàn** 早饭

breast **rǔfáng** 乳房

breathe **hūxī** 呼吸

bridge **qiáo** 桥

bring **ná** 拿

British (in general) **Yīngguóde** 英国的

British (person) **Yīngguórén** 英国人

brochure **xiǎocèzi** 小册子

broken **huàile** 坏了

bronze **tóng/qīngtóng** 铜／青铜

brothel **jìyuàn** 妓院

brother **xiōngdì** 兄弟

brown **hèsè/zōngsè** 褐色／棕色

bruise **qīngzhǒng** 青肿

brush **shuāzi** 刷子

Buddhism **Fójiào** 佛教

building **dàlóu** 大楼

bulb **diàndēngpào** 电灯泡

burglary **dàoqiè** 盗窃

burn (injury) **shāoshāng** 烧伤

burn (verb) **shāo** 烧

bus **gōnggòngqìchē** 公共汽车

bus stop **gōnggòng qìchēzhàn** 公共汽车站

business **shāngyè** 商业

business card **míngpiàn** 名片

business class **tóuděngcāng** 头等舱

business trip **chūchāi** 出差

businessman **shāngrén** 商人

busy (schedule) **máng** 忙

busy (traffic) **yōngjǐ** 拥挤

but **dànshì** 但是

butter **huángyóu** 黄油

button (for clothes) **kòuzi** 扣子

button (to press) **ànniǔ** 按钮

buy **mǎi** 买

by airmail **hángkōng yóujì** 航空邮寄

by phone **dǎ diànhuà** 打电话

c

cabbage **juǎnxīncài** 卷心菜

cabin **kècāng** 客舱

cake **dàn'gāo** 蛋糕

cake shop **gāodiǎndiàn** 糕点店

call (name) **míng jiào** 名叫

call (phone) **dǎ diànhuà** 打电话

calligraphy **shūfǎ** 书法

camera **zhàoxiàngjī** 照相机

camping **yěyíng** 野营

can (be able to) **néng/kěyǐ** 能／可以

can (tin of food) **guàntóu** 罐头

can opener **guàntóudāo** 罐头刀

cancel **qǔxiāo** 取消

candle **làzhú** 蜡烛

candy **tángguǒ** 糖果

Cantonese **Guǎngdōnghuà** 广东话

car **qìchē** 汽车

car seat (child's) **xiǎohái zuòr (qìchē lǐde)** 小孩座儿(汽车里的)

car trouble **qìchē yǒu máobìng** 汽车有毛病

card **míngpiàn** 名片

cardigan **máoyī** 毛衣

care for **zhàogu** 照顾

careful **xiǎoxīn** 小心

carpet **dìtǎn** 地毯

carriage **kèchēxiāng** 客车厢

carrot **húluóbo** 胡萝卜

carry **tí/dài/zài** 提／带／载

cash **xiànkuǎn** 现款

cash a check **duìxiàn** 兑现

cash machine **tíkuǎnjī** 提款机

cashier **chū'nàyuán** 出纳员

casino **dǔchǎng** 赌场

cassette **héshì cídài** 盒式磁带

cat **māo** 猫

catalogue **mùlù** 目录

cauliflower **huācài** 花菜

cause **yuányīn** 原因

cave **yándòng** 岩洞

celebrate **qìngzhù** 庆祝

cemetery **mùdì** 墓地

center (middle) **zhōngjiān** 中间

center (of city) **(shì) zhōngxīn** (市)中心

Centigrade **Shèshì** 摄氏

centimeter **gōngfēn** 公分

central heating **shì'nèi nuǎnqì** 室内暖气

ceramics **táoqì** 陶器

certificate **zhèngshū** 证书

chair **yǐzi** 椅子

champagne **xiāngbīnjiǔ** 香槟酒

chance **jīhuì** 机会

change (alter, vary) **gǎibiàn** 改变

change (money) **língqián** 零钱

change (swap) **jiāohuàn** 交换

change (trains/buses) **zhuǎnchē** 转车

change the baby's diaper **huàn niàobù** 换尿布

charge (expense, cost) **fèiyòng** 费用

charter flight **bāozū de bānjī** 包租的班机

chat **liáotiānr** 聊天儿

cheap **piányi** 便宜

check (bill) **zhàngdān** 帐单

check (money order) **zhīpiào** 支票

check (verb) **jiǎnchá** 检查

check in **dēngjì** 登记

check out **tuìfáng** 退房

checked luggage **jiǎnchá xíngli** 检查行李

Cheers! **Gānbēi!** 干杯!

cheese **rǔlào/nǎilào** 乳酪／奶酪

chef **chúshī** 厨师

chemist (pharmacy) **yàodiàn** 药店

chess **guójì xiàngqí** 国际象棋

chewing gum **kǒuxiāngtáng** 口香糖

chicken **jī** 鸡

child **háizi** 孩子

chilled **bīngzhèn** 冰镇

chilli **làjiāo** 辣椒

chin **xiàba** 下巴

China **Zhōngguó** 中国

Chinese (in general) **Zhōngguóde** 中国的

Chinese (language) **Zhōngwén/ Hànyǔ** 中文／汉语

Chinese (people) **Zhōngguórén** 中国人

chocolate **qiǎokèlì** 巧克力

choose **xuǎnzé** 选择

chop (for name) **yìnzhāng** 印章

chopsticks **kuàizi** 筷子

church **jiàotáng** 教堂

church service **lǐbài** 礼拜

cigar **xuějiāyān** 雪茄烟

cigarette **xiāngyān** 香烟

circle (theater seats) **lóutīng** 楼厅

circus **mǎxì** 马戏

citizen **shìmín/gōngmín** 市民／ 公民

city **chéngshì** 城市

clean **gānjìng** 干净

clean (verb) **nòng gānjìng** 弄干净

clock **shízhōng/zhōng** 时钟／钟

close **jìn/kàojìn** 近／靠近

closed (shop, etc) **guānmén** 关门

closed off (road) **fēngsuǒ** 封锁

clothes, clothing **yīfu** 衣服

clothes hanger **yījià** 衣架

cloud **yún** 云

coach (bus) **chángtúqìchē** 长途汽车

coat (jacket) **wàiyī** 外衣

coat (overcoat) **dàyī** 大衣

cockroach **zhāngláng** 蟑螂

coffee **kāfēi** 咖啡

cold (not hot) **lěng** 冷

cold, flu **gǎnmào** 感冒

collar **yīlǐng** 衣领

colleague **tóngshì** 同事

collision **zhuàngchē** 撞车

cologne **nánxìng xiāngshuǐ** 男性香水

color **yánsè** 颜色

colored **dài yánsè de** 带颜色的

comb **shūzi** 梳子

come **lái** 来

come back **huílai** 回来

comedy **xǐjù** 喜剧

comfortable **shūfu** 舒服

company (business) **gōngsī** 公司

compartment (train) **fēn'géjiān (lièchē chēxiāng de)** 分隔间（列车车厢的）

complain **bàoyuàn** 抱怨

complaint **tóusù** 投诉

completely **quánbù** 全部

complex **fùzá** 复杂

computer **diànnǎo** 电脑

comrade **tóngzhì** 同志

concert **yīnyuèhuì** 音乐会

concert hall **yīnyuètīng** 音乐厅

condensed milk **liànrǔ** 炼乳

condom **bìyùntào** 避孕套

confectionery **tángguǒ** 糖果

confirm **quèrèn** 确认

Congratulations! **Zhùhè nǐ!** 祝贺你!

connection (transport) **liánjiēdiǎn** 连接点

constipation **biànmì** 便秘

consulate **lǐngshìguǎn** 领事馆

consultation (by doctor) **kàn-bìng/jiùzhěn** 看病／就诊

contact lens **yǐnxíng yǎnjìng** 隐型眼镜

contagious **chuánrǎn de** 传染的

contraceptive **bìyùn** 避孕

contraceptive pill **bìyùnyào** 避孕药

contract **hétóng/qìyuē** 合同／契约

convenient **fāngbiàn** 方便

cook (person) **chúshī** 厨师

cook (verb) **zuòcài** 做菜

cookie **xiǎotiánbǐng** 小甜饼

copper **tóng/zǐtóng** 铜／紫铜

copy **fùběn** 副本

copy (verb) **chāoxiě/mófǎng** 抄写／模仿

corner **jiǎoluò** 角落

correct **duì/zhèngquè** 对／正确

correspond **tōngxìn** 通信

corridor **zǒuláng** 走廊

corrupt **fǔbài** 腐败

cosmetics **huàzhuāngpǐn** 化妆品

cost **chéngběn** 成本

cost (price) **jiàgé** 价格

costly **guì/ángguì** 贵／昂贵

costume **mínzú fúzhuāng/xìzhuāng** 民族服装／戏装

cot **yīng'érchuáng/tóngchuáng** 婴儿床／童床

cotton **miánbù** 棉布

cotton wool **miánhuā** 棉花

cough **késoushēng** 咳嗽声

cough (verb) **késou** 咳嗽

cough lolly **késou táng** 咳嗽糖

cough syrup **késou yàoshuǐ** 咳嗽药水

count (verb) **shǔ/suàn** 数／算

counter **guìtái** 柜台

country (nation) **guójiā** 国家

country (rural area) **xiāngxià** 乡下

country code **guójiā qūhào** 国家区号

course of treatment **liáochéng** 疗程

cousin (children of father's brothers) **tángxiōngdìjiěmèi** 堂兄弟姐妹

cousin (children of father's sisters and mother's siblings) **biǎoxiōngdìjiěmèi** 表兄弟姐妹

cover (verb) **gài** 盖

cow **mǔniú** 母牛

crab **pángxiè** 螃蟹

cramp (verb) **chōujīn** 抽筋

crazy **fēngkuángde** 疯狂的

credit card **xìnyòngkǎ** 信用卡

crime **fànzuì** 犯罪

cross (road, river) **yuèguò** 越过

crossroads **shízìlùkǒu** 十字路口

crutch **guǎizhàng** 拐杖

cry **kū** 哭

cubic meter **lìfāngmǐ** 立方米

cucumber **huángguā** 黄瓜

cuddly toy **yǐnrén lǒubào de wánjù** 引人搂抱的玩具

cuff **xiùkǒu** 袖口

cufflinks **(chènshān xiùkǒu de) liànkòu** 〔衬衫袖口的〕链扣

cup **bēizi** 杯子

curly **juǎnqūde** 卷曲的

current (electric) **diànliú** 电流

curtains **chuānglián** 窗帘

cushion **diànzi** 垫子

custom **xísú** 习俗

customer **gùkè** 顾客

customs **hǎiguān** 海关

cut (injury) **shāngkǒu** 伤口

cut (verb) **qiē/gē** 切／割

cutlery **dāochā cānjù** 刀叉餐具

cycling **qí zìxíngchē** 骑自行车

D

dad **bàba** 爸爸

daily **rìchángde** 日常的

dairy products **nǎizhìpǐn** 奶制品

damage (verb) **sǔnhài** 损害

dance (verb) **tiàowǔ** 跳舞

dance **wǔhuì** 舞会

dandruff **tóupíxuè** 头皮屑

danger **wēixiǎn** 危险

dangerous **wēixiǎn de** 危险的

dark **àn/hēi'àn** 暗／黑暗

date **rìqī** 日期

date of birth **chūshēng rìqī** 出生日期

daughter **nǚ'ér** 女儿

day **tiān** 天

day after tomorrow **hòutiān** 后天

day before yesterday **qiántiān** 前天

dead **sǐ le** 死了

deaf **lóngde** 聋的

decaffeinated **wúkāfēiyīn de** 无咖啡因的

deceive **qīpiàn** 欺骗

December **Shí'èryuè** 十二月

decide **juédìng** 决定

declare (customs) **bàoguān** 报关

deep **shēn** 深

deep freeze **jídòng** 急冻

degrees **dù** 度

delay **dān'ge** 耽搁

delicious **hǎochī** 好吃

deliver **yùnsòng** 运送

democracy **mínzhǔ** 民主

dentist **yáyī** 牙医

dentures **jiǎyá** 假牙

deny **fǒurèn** 否认

deodorant **chútǐchòuyè** 除体臭液

department store **bǎihuòshāngdiàn** 百货商店

departure **chūfā** 出发

departure time **qǐchéng shíjiān** 起程时间

deposit (for safekeeping) **yājīn** 押金

deposit (in bank) **cúnkuǎn** 存款

desert **shāmò** 沙漠

dessert **tiánshí** 甜食

destination **mùdìdì** 目的地

destroy **pòhuài** 破坏

detergent **qùgòujì** 去垢剂

develop (photo) **chōngxǐ** 冲洗

diabetic **tángniàobìng** 糖尿病

dial (phone) **bō (diànhuà)** 拨(电话)

diamond **zuànshí** 钻石

diaper **zhǐniàobù** 纸尿布

diarrhea **lā dùzi** 拉肚子

dictionary **cídiǎn** 词典

diesel oil **cháiyóu** 柴油

diet **yǐnshí** 饮食

different **bùtóng** 不同

difficulty **kùnnan** 困难

dim sum **gǎngshì diǎnxīn** 港式点心

dining car **cānchē** 餐车

dining room **cāntīng** 餐厅

dinner **wǎnfàn** 晚饭

direct flight **zhíháng** 直航

direction **fāngxiàng** 方向

directly **zhíjiē** 直接

dirty **zāng** 脏

disabled **cánjirén** 残疾人

disappointment **shīwàng** 失望

disco **dísīkē** 迪斯科

discount **yōuhuì** 优惠

dish **pánzi** 盘子

dish of the day **jīntiān tuījiàn de cài** 今天推荐的菜

disinfectant **xiāodújì** 消毒剂

dislocate **tuōjiù** 脱臼

dissatisfied **bù mǎnyì** 不满意

distance **jùlí** 距离

distilled water **zhēngliúshuǐ** 蒸馏水

disturb **dǎrǎo** 打扰

disturbance **sāoluàn** 骚乱

divorced **líhūn** 离婚

dizzy **tóuyūn** 头晕

do **zuò** 做

do not disturb **qǐng wù dǎrǎo** 请勿打扰

doctor **yīshēng/dàifu** 医生／大夫

dog **gǒu** 狗

doll **wáwa** 娃娃

domestic **guónèi** 国内

door **mén** 门

double **shuāngbèi** 双倍

double bed **shuāngrénchuáng** 双人床

down **xià** 下

downstairs **lóuxià** 楼下

draught **chuāntángfēng** 穿堂风

dream **mèng** 梦

dream (verb) **zuòmèng** 做梦

dress (verb) **chuān** 穿

dress **liányīqún** 连衣裙

dress up **chuānbàn** 穿扮

dressing gown **chényī** 晨衣

dressing table **shūzhuāngtái** 梳妆台

drink (alcoholic) **dài jiǔjīng de yǐnliào** 带酒精的饮料

drink (refreshment) **yǐnliào** 饮料

drink (verb) **hē** 喝

drinking water **yǐnyòngshuǐ** 饮用水

drive (verb) **kāichē** 开车

driver **sījī** 司机

driver's license **jiàshǐzhèng** 驾驶证

drug (medicine) **yào** 药

drug (recreational) **dúpǐn** 毒品

drugstore **yàodiàn** 药店

drunk **hēzuì** 喝醉

dry **gān** 干

dry (verb) **nònggān** 弄干

dry-clean **gānxǐ** 干洗

drycleaners **gānxǐdiàn** 干洗店

duck **yāzi** 鸭子

dumpling **jiǎozi** 饺子

during **zài...qījiān** 在…期间

during the day **báitiān** 白天

dust **huīchén** 灰尘

duty (tax) **guānshuì** 关税

duty-free goods **miǎnshuìpǐn** 免税品

duty-free shop **miǎnshuìdiàn** 免税店

DVD **shùmǎ guāngdié** 数码光碟

dynasty **cháodài** 朝代

182

E

each **měi** 每

each other **hùxiāng** 互相

ear **ěrduo** 耳朵

ear drops **ěryàoshuǐ** 耳药水

earache **ěrduo téng** 耳朵疼

early **zǎo** 早

earn **zhuàn** 赚

earrings **ěrhuán** 耳环

earthquake **dìzhèn** 地震

east **dōngbiān** 东边

easy **róngyì** 容易

eat **chī** 吃

economy **jīngjì** 经济

economy class **jīngjìcāng** 经济舱

egg **jīdàn** 鸡蛋

eggplant **qiézi** 茄子

eight **bā** 八

eighteen **shíbā** 十八

eighty **bāshí** 八十

electric fan **diànfēngshàn** 电风扇

electricity **diàn** 电

electronic **diànzi** 电子

elephant **dàxiàng** 大象

elevator **diàntī** 电梯

eleven **shíyī** 十一

email **diànzi yóujiàn** 电子邮件

embarrassed **nánwéiqíng** 难为情

embassy **dàshǐguǎn** 大使馆

embroidery **cìxiù** 刺绣

emergency **jízhěn** 急诊

emergency brake **jǐnjí shāchē** 紧急刹车

emergency exit **jǐnjí chūkǒu** 紧急出口

emperor **huāngdì** 皇帝

empress **huānghòu** 皇后

empty **kōngde** 空的

end **wán** 完

English (language) **Yīngwén/ Yīngyǔ** 英文／英语

enjoy **xiǎngshòu** 享受

enough **zúgòu** 足够

enquire **wèn** 问

enter **jìnrù** 进入

entire **quánbù** 全部

entrance **rùkǒu** 入口

envelope **xìnfēng** 信封

equality **píngděng** 平等

escalator **diàndòng fútī** 电动扶梯

especially **tèbié** 特别

essential **zhòngyào** 重要

evening **wǎnshang** 晚上

evening wear **wǎnzhuāng** 晚装

every **měi** 每

everybody **měi ge rén** 每个人

everything **yíqiè** 一切

everywhere **dàochù** 到处

examine **jiǎnchá** 检查

example **lìzi** 例子

excellent **yōuxiù de** 优秀的

exchange (money) **duìhuàn** 兑换

exchange rate **duìhuànlǜ** 兑换率

excursion **duǎntú lǚxíng** 短途旅行

excuse me **qǐngwèn** 请问

exhausted **lèihuàile** 累坏了

exhibition **zhǎnlǎn** 展览

exit, export **chūkǒu** 出口

expenses **fèiyòng** 费用

expensive **guì** 贵

explain **jiěshì** 解释

express (letter) **kuàidì** 快递

express (train) **tèkuài** 特快

external use **wàiyòng de** 外用的

extension cord **jiēcháng diànxiàn** 接长电线

eye **yǎnjing** 眼睛

eye drops **yǎnyàoshuǐ** 眼药水

eye specialist **yǎnkē yīshēng** 眼科医生

F

fabric **bùliào** 布料

face **liǎn** 脸

factory **gōngchǎng** 工厂

Fahrenheit **Huáshì** 华氏

faint **hūnjué** 昏厥

fall (season) **qiūtiān** 秋天

fall (verb) **dǎoxiàlái** 倒下来

false **jiǎde** 假的

family **jiātíng** 家庭

famous **yǒumíng** 有名

fan **shànzi** 扇子

far away **hěn yuǎn** 很远

fare **piào jià** 票价

farm **nóngcǎng** 农场

farmer **nóngfū** 农夫

fashion show **shízhuāng biǎoyǎn** 时装表演

fast **kuài** 快

fat **pàng** 胖

father **fùqin/bàba** 父亲／爸爸

father-in-law **yuèfù** 岳父

fault **guòcuò** 过错

fax **chuánzhēn** 传真

February **Èryuè** 二月

feel **juéde** 觉得

feel like **xiǎng yào** 想要

fence **líbā** 篱笆

ferry **dùchuán** 渡船

festival **jiérì** 节日

fever **fāshāo** 发烧

few **jíshǎo/jǐge** 极少／几个

few (number) **jǐ ge** 几个

fiancè **wèihūnfū** 未婚夫

fiancèe **wèihūnqī** 未婚妻

fifteen **shíwǔ** 十五

fifty **wǔshí** 五十

fill (verb) **zhuāngmǎn** 装满

fill out (form) **tiánbiǎo** 填表

filling (dental) **tiánchōngwù** 填充物

film (cinema) 电影 **diànyǐng**

film (photo) **jiāojuǎn** 胶卷

filter (lens) **lǜguāngqì** 滤光气

filter cigarette **xiāngyān guòlǜzuǐ** 香烟过滤嘴

find **zhǎo** 找

fine (money) **fákuǎn** 罚款

fine food **měicān** 美餐

finger **shǒuzhǐ** 手指

finish **wánchéng** 完成

fire **shīhuǒ** 失火

fire alarm **huǒjǐng** 火警

fire department **xiāofángjú** 消防局

fire escape **ānquántī** 安全梯

fire extinguisher **mièhuǒqì** 灭火器

first **dìyī** 第一

first aid **jíjiù** 急救

first class **tóuděngzuò** 头等座

fish **yú** 鱼

fish (verb) **diàoyú** 钓鱼

fishing rod **yúgān** 鱼竿

fitness club **jiànshēn jùlèbù** 健身俱乐部

fitness training **jiànshēn duànliàn** 健身锻炼

fitting room **shìyīshì** 试衣室

five **wǔ** 五

fix **xiūlǐ** 修理

flag **qí** 旗

flash (camera) **shǎnguāngdēng** 闪光灯

flashlight **shǒudiàntǒng** 手电筒

flavor **wèidào** 味道

flight **bānjī** 班机

flight number **bānjīhào** 班机号

flood **hóngshuǐ** 洪水

floor **lóu/céng** 楼／层

flour **miànfěn** 面粉

flu **gǎnmào** 感冒

flush **chōngxǐ** 冲洗

fly (insect) **cāngyíng** 苍蝇

fly (verb) **fēi** 飞

fog **wù** 雾

foggy **qǐwù** 起雾

folklore **mínsú** 民俗

follow **gēnsuí** 跟随

food (groceries) **shíwù** 食物

food (meal) **fàncài** 饭菜

food poisoning **shíwù zhòngdú** 食物中毒

foot (anatomy) **jiǎo** 脚

football (soccer) **zúqiú** 足球

forbidden **jìnzhǐ** 禁止

foreign **wàiguó de** 外国的

foreign exchange **wàihuì** 外汇

forget **wàngjì** 忘记

fork **chāzi** 叉子

form **biǎogé** 表格

formal dress **wǎnlǐfú** 晚礼服

forty **sìshí** 四十

forward **xiàng qián** 向前

four **sì** 四

France **Fǎguó** 法国

free (no charge) **miǎnfèi** 免费

free (unoccupied) **yǒu kòngr** 有空儿

free time **kòngr** 空儿

freedom **zìyóu** 自由

freeze **jiébīng** 结冰

French (in general) **Fǎguóde** 法国的

French (language) **Fǎyǔ/Fǎwén** 法语／法文

French (people) **Fǎguórén** 法国人

french fries **zháshǔtiáo** 炸薯条

fresh **xīnxiān** 新鲜

Friday **Xīngqíwǔ** 星期五

fried **yóuzhá** 油炸

friend **péngyou** 朋友

friendly **yǒuhǎo** 友好

frightened **bèixiàzhe** 被吓着

fringe (hair) **qián liúhǎir** 前刘海儿

from **cóng** 从

front **qiánmiàn** 前面

frozen **bīngdòng** 冰冻

fruit **shuǐguǒ** 水果

fruit juice **guǒzhī** 果汁

frying pan **jiān'guō** 煎锅

full **mǎn** 满

fun **hǎowánr** 好玩儿

funeral **zànglǐ** 葬礼

funny **hǎoxiào** 好笑

G

game **yóuxì** 游戏

garage (car repair) **xiūchēxíng** 修车行

garbage **lājī** 垃圾

garden **huāyuán** 花园

garlic **dàsuàn** 大蒜

garment **yīfu** 衣服

gas station **jiāyóuzhàn** 加油站

gasoline **qìyóu** 汽油

gate **dàmén** 大门

gem **bǎoshí** 宝石

gender **xìngbié** 性别

genuine **zhēnde** 真的

German (language) **Déyǔ/ Déwén** 德语／德文

German (in general) **Déguó de** 德国的

German (people) **Déguórén** 德国人

Germany **Déguó** 德国

get off (boat) **xiàchuán** 下船

get off (bus, train) **xiàchē** 下车

get on (boat) **shàngchuán** 上船

get on (bus, train) **shàngchē** 上车

gift **lǐwù** 礼物

ginger **jiāng** 姜

girl **nǚháir/gūniang** 女孩儿／姑娘

girlfriend **nǚpéngyou** 女朋友

give **gěi** 给

given name **míngzi** 名字

glass (for drinking) **bēizi** 杯子

glass (material) **bōli** 玻璃

glasses **yǎnjìng** 眼镜

glossy (photo) **guāngmiàn de** 光面的

gloves **shǒutào** 手套

glue **jiāoshuǐ** 胶水

go **qù** 去

go back **huíqù** 回去

go out **chūqù** 出去

gold **jīn** 金

golf **gāo'ěrfūqiú** 高尔夫球

golf course **gāo'ěrfūqiú chǎng** 高尔夫球场

good afternoon **xiàwǔhǎo** 下午好

good evening **wǎnshàng hǎo** 晚上好

good morning **zǎoshang hǎo** 早上好

good night **wǎn'ān** 晚安

goodbye **zàijiàn** 再见

gram **kè** 克

grandchild **sūnzǐ** 孙子

granddaughter **sūnnǚ** 孙女

grandfather (maternal) **wàizǔfù/ lǎoye** 外祖父／姥爷

grandfather (paternal) **zǔfù/ yéye** 祖父／爷爷

grandmother (maternal) **wàizǔmǔ/lǎolao** 外祖母／姥姥

grandmother (paternal) **zǔmǔ/ nǎinai** 祖母／奶奶

grandparent (maternal) **wàizǔfùmǔ** 外祖父母

grandparent (paternal) **zǔfùmǔ** 祖父母

grandson **sūn'ér** 孙儿

grapes **pútao** 葡萄

grave **fénmù** 坟墓

gray **huīsè** 灰色

gray-haired **huībái** 灰白

graze (injury) **cāpòchù** 擦破处

greasy (food) **yóunì** 油腻

Great Britain **Yīngguó** 英国

Great Wall **Chángchéng** 长城

green **lǜsè** 绿色

green tea **lǜchá** 绿茶

greengrocer **shūcài-shuǐguǒdiàn** 蔬菜水果店

greeting **dǎ zhāohu** 打招呼

grilled **shāokǎo** 烧烤

groceries **záhuò** 杂货

grocery **záhuòdiàn** 杂货店

group **tuántǐ** 团体

guide (book) **lǚyóu zhǐnán** 旅游指南

guide (person) **dǎoyóu** 导游

guided tour **jiěshuō de cānguān** 解说的参观

guilty **yǒuzuì** 有罪

gym **jiànshēnfáng** 健身房

gynecologist **fùkē yīshēng** 妇科医生

H

hair **tóufa** 头发

hairbrush **shūzi** 梳子

haircut **lǐfà** 理发

hairdresser **lǐfàshī** 理发师

hairdryer **chuīfēngjī** 吹风机

hairspray **dìngxíngjiāo** 定型胶

hairstyle **fàxíng** 发型

half **yíbàn** 一半

half full **bànmǎn** 半满

ham **huǒtuǐ** 火腿

hand **shǒu** 手

hand brake **shǒuzhá** 手闸

hand luggage **shǒutí xíngli** 手提行李

hand towel **shǒujīn** 手巾

handbag **shǒutíbāo** 手提包

handkerchief **shǒujuànr** 手绢儿

handmade **shǒugōngzhì de** 手工制的

handsome **yīngjùn** 英俊

hanger **yījià** 衣架

happy **kāixīn, gāoxìng** 开心，高兴

harbor **gǎngkǒu** 港口

hard (difficult) **nán** 难

hard (firm) **yìng** 硬

hard seat (train) **yìngzuò** 硬座

hard berth (train) **yìngwò** 硬卧

hat **màozi** 帽子

have **yǒu** 有

have to **bìxū** 必需

hay fever **huāfěnrè** 花粉热

he **tā** 他

head **tóu** 头

headache **tóuténg** 头疼

headlights **qiándēng** 前灯

healthy **jiànkāng** 健康

hear **tīngjiàn** 听见

hearing aid **zhùtīngqì** 助听器

heart **xīnzàng** 心脏

heart attack **xīnzàngbìng** 心脏病

heat **nuǎnqì** 暖气

heater **nuǎnlú** 暖炉

heavy **zhòng** 重

heel (of foot) **jiǎohòugēn** 脚后跟

heel (of shoe) **hòugēn** 后跟

height **gāodù** 高度

height (body) **shēn'gāo** 身高

hello **Nǐ hǎo** 你好

help (assist) **bāngzhù/bāngmáng** 帮助／帮忙

Help! (for emergency) **Jiùmìng ā!** 救命阿！

helping (of food) **(shíwù de) yífèn** （食物的）一份

here **zhèlǐ/zhèr** 这里／这儿

high **gāo** 高

high chair **gāoyǐ** 高椅

high tide **gāocháo** 高潮

highway **gōnglù** 公路

hiking **túbù lǚxíng** 徒步旅行

hire **zū** 租

history **lìshǐ** 历史

hitchhike **dāchē** 搭车

hobby **àihào** 爱好

holiday (festival) **jiérì** 节日

holiday (public) **jiàrì** 假日

holiday (vacation) **dùjià** 度假

homesick **xiǎngjiā** 想家

homosexual **tóngxìngliàn** 同性恋

honest **chéngshí de** 诚实的

honey **fēngmì** 蜂蜜

hope **xīwàng** 希望

horrible **kěpà de** 可怕的

hors d'oeuvres **kāiwèicài** 开胃菜

horse **mǎ** 马

hospital **yīyuàn** 医院

hospitality **hàokè** 好客

hot (spicy) **là** 辣

hot (warm) **rè** 热

hot spring **wēnquán** 温泉

hot water **rèshuǐ** 热水

hot-water bottle **nuǎnshuǐdài** 暖水袋

hotel **lǚguǎn/bīn'guǎn** 旅馆／宾馆

hour **xiǎoshí/zhōngtóu** 小时／钟头

house **fángzi** 房子

how **zěnme** 怎么

How far? **Duō yuǎn?** 多远?

How long? **Duō cháng?** 多长?

How many? **Duōshao/jǐ ge?** 多少／几个?

How much? **Duōshao qián?** 多少钱?

humid **cháoshī** 潮湿

hundred **bǎi** 百

hungry **è** 饿

hurry (pressed) **jí** 急

hurry (quickly) **gǎnkuài** 赶快

husband **zhàngfū** 丈夫

I

I **wǒ** 我

ice **bīng** 冰

ice cream **bīngjīlíng/bīngqílín** 冰激凌／冰淇淋

ice-skating **huábīng** 滑冰

idea **zhǔyì** 主意

identification (card) **shēnfènzhèng** 身份证

identify **shēnfèn** 身份

idiot **báichī** 白痴

if **rúguǒ/yàoshi** 如果／要是

ill **yǒubìng de** 有病的

illegal **fēifǎ** 非法

illness **bìng** 病

imagine **xiǎngxiàng** 想象

immediately **lìkè/mǎshàng** 立刻／马上

immigration/arrival **rùjìng** 入境

important **zhòngyào** 重要

impossible **bù kěnéng** 不可能

improve **gǎijìn** 改进

in **zài...lǐ** 在…里

in the evening **zài wǎnshang** 在晚上

in the morning **zài zǎoshàng** 在早上

increase **zēngjiā** 增加

included **bāokuò zài nèi** 包括在内

including **bāokuò** 包括

income **shōurù** 收入

indicate **zhǐshì** 指示

indicator (car) **zhǐshìqì** 指示器

indigestion **xiāohuà bù liáng** 消化不良

inexpensive **piányi** 便宜

infected **gǎnrǎn** 感染

infectious **chuánrǎn** 传染

inflammation **fāyán** 发炎

inflation **tōnghuò péngzhàng** 通货膨胀

information **xìnxī** 信息

information desk **xúnwèn chù** 询问处

injection **dǎzhēn** 打针

injured **shòushāng** 受伤

innocent **wúgū** 无辜

insect **chóngzǐ** 虫子

insect bite **chóng yǎo** 虫咬

insect repellent **qūchóngjì** 驱虫剂

inside **zài...lǐ** 在…里

instead of **dàitì** 代替

instructions **shuōmíng** 说明

insurance **bǎoxiǎn** 保险

intelligent **cōngmíng** 聪明

interested **gǎn xìngqù** 感兴趣

interesting **yǒuqù** 有趣

internal use (medicine) **nèifú** 内服

international **guójì** 国际

Internet **Hùliánwǎng/wǎngluò** 互联网／网络

Internet cafe, cybercafe **Wǎngbā** 网吧

interpreter **fānyì/kǒuyìyuán** 翻译／口译员

intersection **shízìlùkǒu** 十字路口

introduce **jièshào** 介绍

introduce oneself **zìwǒ jièshào** 自我介绍

invite **yāoqǐng** 邀请

invoice **fāpiào** 发票

Ireland **Ài'ěrlán** 爱尔兰

iron (for clothes) **yùndǒu** 熨斗

iron (metal) **tiě** 铁

iron (verb) **yùn** 熨

island **dǎo** 岛

Italian (in general) **Yìdàlìde** 意大利的

Italian (language) **Yìdàlìyǔ** 意大利语

Italian (people) **Yìdàlìrén** 意大利人

Italy **Yìdàlì** 意大利

itchy **yǎng** 痒

itinerary **rìchéngbiǎo** 日程表

J

jack (for car) **qiānjīndǐng** 千斤顶

jack (verb) **dǐngqǐ** 顶起

jacket **wàitào** 外套

jade **yù** 玉

jam **guǒjiàng** 果酱

January **Yīyuè** 一月

Japan **Rìběn** 日本

Japanese (in general) **Rìběnde** 日本的

Japanese (language) **Rìwén/Rìyǔ** 日文／日语

Japanese (people) **Rìběnrén** 日本人

jasmine tea **mòlì huāchá** 茉莉花茶

jazz **juéshì yīnyuè** 爵士音乐

jeans **niúzǎikù** 牛仔裤

jellyfish **shuǐmǔ** 水母

jewelry **zhūbǎo/shǒushì** 珠宝／首饰

jewelry shop **zhūbǎodiàn** 珠宝店

job **gōngzuò** 工作

jog **pǎobù** 跑步

joke **xiàohuà** 笑话

journalist **jìzhě** 记者

journey **lùtú** 路途

juice **guǒzhī** 果汁

July **Qīyuè** 七月
jumper **máoyī** 毛衣
June **Liùyuè** 六月
just (only) **zhǐ** 只
just (very recently) **gāngcái** 刚才

K

keep **liú** 留
kerosene **méiyóu** 煤油
key **yàoshi** 钥匙
kilogram **gōngjīn** 公斤
kilometer **gōnglǐ** 公里
king **guówáng** 国王
kitchen **chúfáng** 厨房
knee **xīgài** 膝盖
knife **dāozi** 刀子
knit **dǎ máoyī** 打毛衣
know (facts) **zhīdào** 知道
know (people) **rènshi** 认识

L

laces (for shoes) **xiédài** 鞋带
lake **hú** 湖
lamb (mutton) **yángròu** 羊肉
lamp **dēng** 灯
land (ground) **dì** 地
land (verb) **zhuólù** 着陆
landscape **fēngjǐng** 风景
lane (of traffic) **lùxiàn** 路线
language **yǔyán** 语言
large **dà** 大
last (endure) **chíxù** 持续
last (final) **zuìhòu** 最后
last night **zuówǎn** 昨晚
late **wǎn** 晚
late in arriving **chídào** 迟到
later **guò yìhuǐr** 过一会儿
laugh **xiào** 笑

launderette **xǐyīdiàn** 洗衣店
laundry soap **xǐyīfěn** 洗衣粉
law **fǎlǜ** 法律
lawyer **lǜshī** 律师
laxative **qīngxièjì** 轻泻剂
lazy **lǎnduò** 懒惰
leaded petrol **hánqiān qìyóu** 含铅汽油
leak **lòushuǐ** 漏水
learn **xué** 学
leather **pígé** 皮革
leave **líkāi** 离开
leave (train/bus) **kāichē** 开车
least **zuìshǎo** 最少
least (at least) **zhìshǎo/qǐmǎ** 至少/起码
left (direction) **zuǒbiān** 左边
left behind **liúxià** 留下
leg **tuǐ** 腿
legal **héfǎ** 合法
leisure **kōngxián** 空闲
lemon **níngméng** 柠檬
lend **jiè** 借
lens (camera) **jìngtóu** 镜头
less **shǎo yìdiǎnr** 少一点儿
letter **xìn** 信
letter-writing paper **xìnzhǐ** 信纸
lettuce **wōjù** 莴苣
library **túshūguǎn** 图书馆
license **zhízhào** 执照
lie (be lying) **shuōhuǎng** 说谎
lie (falsehood) **huǎnghuà** 谎话
lie down **tǎngxià** 躺下
lift (elevator) **diàntī** 电梯
light (lamp) **dēng** 灯
light (not dark) **liàng** 亮
light (not heavy) **qīng** 轻
light bulb **dēngpào** 灯泡

lighter **dǎhuǒjī** 打火机

lightning **shǎndiàn** 闪电

like (verb) **xǐhuan** 喜欢

linen **chuángdān** 床单

lip **zuǐchún** 嘴唇

lipstick **kǒuhóng** 口红

listen **tīng** 听

liter **shēng** 升

little (amount) **yìdiǎnr** 一点儿

little (small) **xiǎo** 小

live (alive) **huózhe** 活着

live (verb) **shēnghuó** 生活

liver **gān** 肝

lobster **lóngxiā** 龙虾

local **běndì** 本地

lock **suǒ** 锁

long **cháng** 长

long-distance call **chángtú diàn-huà** 长途电话

look at **kàn** 看

look for **zhǎo** 找

look up **chá** 查

lose (not win) **shū** 输

loss **sǔnshī** 损失

lost (can't find way) **mílù** 迷路

lost (missing) **diūle** 丢了

lost and found office **shīwù zhāolǐngchù** 失物招领处

loud **dàshēng** 大声

love **àiqíng** 爱情

love (verb) **ài** 爱

low **dī** 低

low tide **dīcháo** 低潮

LPG **Méiqì/Shíyóuqì** 煤气／石油气

luck **yùnqì** 运气

luggage **xíngli** 行李

luggage locker **xíngli cúnguì** 行李存柜

lunch **wǔfàn** 午饭

lungs **fèi** 肺

lychees **lìzhī** 荔枝

M

magazine **zázhì** 杂志

mail (letters) **xìn** 信

mail (verb) **jì** 寄

mailbox **yóutǒng** 邮筒

main **zhǔyào** 主要

main road **zhǔgànlù** 主干路

make, create **zuò/zhìzào** 做／制造

make an appointment **yùyuē** 预约

make love **zuò'ài** 做爱

makeshift **línshí còuhuo** 临时凑合

makeup **huàzhuāngpǐn** 化妆品

man **nánrén** 男人

manager **jīnglǐ** 经理

Mandarin (language) **Pǔtōnghuà/Guóyǔ** 普通话／国语

manicure **xiūjiǎ** 修甲

many **hěnduō** 很多

map **dìtú** 地图

March **Sānyuè** 三月

marital status **hūnyīn zhuàngtài** 婚姻状态

market **shìchǎng** 市场

married **yǐhūn** 已婚

massage **ànmó** 按摩

match **bǐsài** 比赛

matches **huǒchái** 火柴

matte (photo) **yǎguāngdede** 哑光的

mattress **chuángdiàn** 床垫

May **Wǔyuè** 五月

maybe **yěxǔ** 也许

meal **cān** 餐

meaning **yìsi** 意思

measure (verb) **liáng** 量

meat **ròu** 肉

medicine **yào** 药

meet **jiànmiàn** 见面

meeting **huìyì** 会议

mend **xiūbǔ** 修补

menu **càidān** 菜单

merchant **shāngrén** 商人

message **liúyán/biàntiáo** 留言／便条

metal **jīnshǔ** 金属

metal detector **jīnshǔ tàncè mén** 金属探测门

meter (in taxi) **jìchéngqì** 计程器

meter (measure) **(yī) mǐ/gōngchǐ** （一）米／公尺

method **fāngfǎ** 方法

midday **zhōngwǔ** 中午

middle **zhōngjiān** 中间

midnight **wǔyè** 午夜

migraine **piāntóutòng** 偏头痛

mild (climate) **wēnnuǎn de** 温暖的

milk **niúnǎi** 牛奶

millimeter **háomǐ** 毫米

million **bǎiwàn** 百万

mine **wǒde** 我的

mineral water **kuàngquánshuǐ** 矿泉水

minute **fēn (zhōng)** 分（钟）

mirror **jìngzi** 镜子

miss (flight, train) **méi gǎnshàng** 没赶上

Miss (term of address) **xiǎojie** 小姐

miss (think of) **xiǎngniàn** 想念

missing **shīzōngle** 失踪了

missing person **shīzōngzhě** 失踪者

mist **bówù** 薄雾

misty **yǒu bówù** 有薄雾

mistake **cuòwù** 错误

mistaken **nòngcuò** 弄错

misunderstanding **wùhuì** 误会

modern **xiàndàide** 现代的

Monday **Xīngqíyī** 星期一

money **qián** 钱

monkey **hóuzi** 猴子

month **yuè** 月

moon **yuèliang** 月亮

moped **jīdòng zìxíngchē** 机动自行车

morning **zǎoshang** 早上

more **duō yìdiǎnr** 多一点儿

mosquito **wénzi** 蚊子

mosquito net **wénzhàng** 蚊帐

mother **māma/mǔqīn** 妈妈／母亲

mother-in-law **yuèmǔ** 岳母

motorbike **mótuōchē** 摩托车

mountain **shān** 山

mouse **xiǎolǎoshǔ** 小老鼠

mouth **zuǐ** 嘴

move (heavy object) **bān** 搬

movie **diànyǐng** 电影

Mr. **xiānsheng** 先生

Mrs **tàitai** 太太

MSG **wèijīng** 味精

much **xǔduō** 许多

mud **ní** 泥

muscle **jīròu** 肌肉

museum **bówùguǎn** 博物馆

mushrooms **mógu** 蘑菇

music **yīnyuè** 音乐

musical instrument **yuèqì** 乐器

Muslim **Qīngzhēn/Mùsīlín/ Huíjiào** 清真／穆斯林／回教

must **bìxū** 必须

mutton **yángròu** 羊肉

my **wǒde** 我的

N

nail (finger) **zhǐjiǎ** 指甲

nail (metal) **dīngzi** 钉子

nail clippers **zhǐjiǎqián** 指甲钳

nail file **zhǐjiǎcuò** 指甲锉

nail scissors **zhǐjiǎjiǎn** 指甲剪

napkin **cānjīn** 餐巾

nappy, diaper **niàobù** 尿布

nationality **guójí** 国籍

natural **zìránde** 自然的

nature **zìránjiè** 自然界

nauseous **zuò'ǒu** 作呕

near **lí...jìn** 离…近

nearby **fùjìn** 附近

necessary **bìxū** 必需

neck **bózi** 脖子

necklace **xiàngliàn** 项链

necktie **lǐngdài** 领带

needle **zhēn** 针

neighbor **línjū** 邻居

nephew (son of a man's brothers) **zhízi/zhí'ér** 侄子／侄儿

nephew (son of a man's sisters or of a woman's siblings) **wàishēng** 外甥

never **cónglái méiyǒu** 从来没有

new **xīn** 新

news **xīnwén** 新闻

newsstand **bàotíng** 报亭

newspaper **bào** 报

next **xià yí ge** 下一个

next to **pángbiān** 旁边

nice **hǎo** 好

niece (daughter of a man's brothers) **zhínǚ** 侄女

niece (daughter of a man's sisters or of a woman's siblings) **wàishēngnǚ** 外甥女

night **yèlǐ** 夜里

night view **yèjǐng** 夜景

nightclub **yèzǒnghuì** 夜总会

nine **jiǔ** 九

nineteen **shíjiǔ** 十九

ninety **jiǔshí** 九十

nipple (bottle) **xiàngpí nǎitóu** 橡皮奶头

no **búshì** 不是

no entry **bùzhǔn shǐrù** 不准驶入

no one **méiyǒu rén** 没有人

no, thank you 不用了，谢谢 **búyòngle, xièxie**

noise **cáozáshēng/zàoyīn** 嘈杂声／噪音

noisy **cáozáde** 嘈杂的

non-stop (flight) **zhíháng** 直航

noodles **miàntiáo** 面条

noon **zhōngwǔ** 中午

normal **zhèngchángde** 正常的

north **běibiān** 北边

nose **bízi** 鼻子

nose drops **bíyàoshuǐ** 鼻药水

nosebleed **bí chūxiě** 鼻出血

notebook **bǐjìběn** 笔记本

notepad **xìnzhǐ** 信纸

nothing **méiyǒu dōngxi** 没有东西

novel **xiǎoshuō** 小说

November **Shíyīyuè** 十一月

now **xiànzài** 现在

number **hàomǎ** 号码

number plate **chēpái hàomǎ** 车牌号码

nurse **hùshì** 护士

O

obvious **míngxiǎn** 明显

occupation **zhíyè** 职业

October **Shíyuè** 十月

of course **dāngrán** 当然

off (gone bad) **huàile** 坏了

off (turned off) **guānshàng** 关上

office **bàn'gōngshì** 办公室

oil **yóu** 油

ointment **yàogāo** 药膏

okay **xíng** 行

old (used for people) **lǎo** 老

old (used for things) **jiù** 旧

Olympics **Àolínpǐkè Yùndònghuì/Àoyùnhuì** 奥林匹克运动会／奥运会

on, at **zài...shàng** 在…上

on (turned on) **kāi** 开

on the left **zài...zuǒbiān** 在…左边

on the right **zài...yòubiān** 在…右边

on the way **kuài dào le** 快到了

once **yí cì** 一次

one **yī** 一

one-way ticket **dānchéngpiào** 单程票

one-way traffic **dānxíngdào** 单行道

onion **yángcōng** 洋葱

online chat **zài xiàn shàng liáotiān** 在线上聊天

only **zhǐyǒu** 只有

open **kāimén** 开门

open (verb) **dǎkāi** 打开

opera **gējù** 歌剧

operate (surgeon) **zuò shǒushù** 做手术

operator (telephone) **zǒngjī** 总机

opportunity **jīhuì** 机会

opposite **duìmiàn** 对面

optician **yǎnjìngshāng** 眼镜商

orange (color) **chéngsè** 橙色

orange (fruit) **júzi** 桔子

order (meal) **diǎncài** 点菜

ordinary **pǔtōng de** 普通的

other **biéde/qítāde** 别的／其他的

other (alternative) **lìngwài** 另外

our **wǒmende** 我们的

outside **wàimiàn** 外面

over there **nàbiān** 那边

overseas **guówài** 国外

overtake (vehicle) **chāochē** 超车

owe **qiàn** 欠

P

packed lunch **fànhé** 饭盒

packet **bāo** 包

page **yè** 页

pagoda **bǎotǎ** 宝塔

pain **tòng** 痛

painkiller **zhǐtòngyào** 止痛药

painting **huàr/huìhuà** 画儿／绘画

pair **yì shuāng** 一双

pajamas **shuìyī** 睡衣

palace **gōngdiàn** 宫殿

pan **guō** 锅

panties **nèikù** 内裤

pants **kùzi** 裤子

pantyhose **wàkù** 袜裤

paper **zhǐ** 纸

parcel **bāoguǒ** 包裹

parents **fùmǔ** 父母

park, gardens **gōngyuán** 公园

parking space **tíngchē wèizi** 停车位子

partner **bànlǚ/huǒbàn** 伴侣／伙伴

party (event) **jùhuì** 聚会

passenger **chéngkè** 乘客

passport **hùzhào** 护照

passport number **hùzhào hàomǎ** 护照号码

pay (verb) **fùqián** 付钱

pay the bill **fùzhàng/mǎidān** 付账／买单

peach **táozi** 桃子

peanut **huāshēng mǐ** 花生米

pear **lí** 梨

pearl **zhēnzhū** 珍珠

peas **wāndòu** 豌豆

pedestrian crossing **rénxíng héngdào** 人行横道

pen **gāngbǐ** 钢笔

pencil **qiānbǐ** 铅笔

penis **yīnjīng** 阴茎

penknife **xiǎodāo** 小刀

people **rén** 人

pepper (black) **hújiāo** 胡椒

pepper (chilli) **làjiāo** 辣椒

performance **yǎnchū** 演出

perfume **xiāngshuǐ** 香水

perhaps **yěxǔ** 也许

period (menstruation) **yuèjīng qī** 月经期

permit **xǔkě zhèng** 许可证

permit (verb) **xǔ/zhǔnxǔ** 许／准许

person **rén** 人

personal **sīrénde** 私人的

perspire **chūhàn** 出汗

petrol **qìyóu** 汽油

petrol station **jiāyóuzhàn** 加油站

pharmacy **yàodiàn** 药店

phone **diànhuà** 电话

phone (verb) **dǎ diànhuà** 打电话

phone booth **gōngyòng diàn-huàtíng** 公用电话亭

phone card **diànhuà cíkǎ** 电话磁卡

phone directory **diànhuàběn** 电话本

phone number **diànhuà hàomǎ** 电话号码

photo **zhàopiàn** 照片

photocopier **fùyìnjī** 复印机

photocopy (verb) **fùyìn** 复印

phrasebook **duǎnyǔjí** 短语集

pick up (someone) **jiē** 接

picnic **yěcān** 野餐

pill (contraceptive) **bìyùnyào** 避孕药

pillow **zhěntou** 枕头

pillowcase **zhěntào** 枕套

pills, tablets **yàowán/yàopiàn** 药丸／药片

pin **dàtóuzhēn** 大头针

pineapple **bōluó** 菠萝

pink **fěnhóngsè** 粉红色

pity **kěxī** 可惜

place **dìfang** 地方

place of interest **míngshèng** 名胜

plain (simple) **pǔsù** 朴素

plan (intention) **dǎsuàn** 打算

plan (map) **gàitú** 概图

plane **fēijī** 飞机

plant **zhíwù** 植物

plastic **sùliào** 塑料

plastic bag **sùliàodài** 塑料袋

plate **pánzi** 盘子

platform **yuètái/zhàntái** 月台／站台

play (drama) **huàjù** 话剧

play (verb) **wánr** 玩儿

play golf **dǎ gāo'ěrfūqiú** 打高尔夫球

play tennis **dǎ wǎngqiú** 打网球

playground **yùndòngchǎng** 运动场

playing cards **pūkèpái** 扑克牌

please **qǐng** 请

plug (electric) **chātóu** 插头

plum **lǐzi** 李子

pocket **kǒudài** 口袋

pocketknife **xiǎozhédāo** 小折刀

point out **zhǐchū** 指出

poisonous **yǒudúde** 有毒的

police **jǐngchá** 警察

police station **gōng'ān jú/jǐngchájú** 公安局／警察局

pond **chítáng** 池塘

pool **yóuyǒngchí** 游泳池

poor (not rich) **qióng** 穷

poor (pitiful) **kělián** 可怜

population **rénkǒu** 人口

porcelain **cíqì** 瓷器

pork **zhūròu** 猪肉

portable power **yídòng diànyuán** 移动电源

portable Wi-Fi router **wúxiàn lùyóuqì** 移动无限路由器

porter (for bags) **fúwùyuán** 服务员

possible **kěnéng** 可能

post (verb) **jì** 寄

post office **yóujú** 邮局

postage **yóufèi** 邮费

postbox **yóutǒng** 邮筒

postcard **míngxìnpiàn** 明信片

postcode **yóuzhèng biānmǎ** 邮政编码

postpone **yánqī** 延期

potato **tǔdòu** 土豆

potato chips **zháshǔtiáo** 炸薯条

poultry **jiāqín** 家禽

powdered milk **nǎifěn** 奶粉

practice **liànxí** 练习

prawn **xiā** 虾

precious stone **bǎoshí** 宝石

prefer **gèng xǐhuan** 更喜欢

preference **xǐ'ài** 喜爱

pregnant **huáiyùn** 怀孕

prepare **zhǔnbèi** 准备

prescription **yàofāng** 药方

present (gift) **lǐwù** 礼物

present (here) **xiànzài** 现在

pressure **yālì** 压力

pretty **piàoliang** 漂亮

price **jiàqián** 价钱

price list **jiàgébiǎo** 价格表

print (picture) **zhàopiàn** 照片

print (from computer) **dǎyìn** 打印

print (develop photo) **(shài) yìn** (晒)印

private **sīrénde** 私人的

probably **dàgài** 大概

problem **wèntí** 问题

product **chǎnpǐn** 产品

profession **zhíyè** 职业

profit **lìrùn** 利润

program **jiémù** 节目

promise **dāyìng** 答应

pronounce **fāyīn** 发音

prostitute **jìnǚ** 妓女

protect **bǎohù** 保护

province **shěng** 省

public **gōnggòng** 公共

pull **lā** 拉

pull a muscle **chěshāng jīròu** 扯伤肌肉

purchase **mǎi** 买

pure **chúnde** 纯的

purple **zǐsè** 紫色

purse (for money) **qiánbāo** 钱包

purse (handbag) **shǒudài** 手袋

push **tuī** 推

put **fàng** 放

pyjamas **shuìyī** 睡衣

Q

quality **zhìliàng** 质量

quantity **shùliàng** 数量

quarrel **chǎojià** 吵架

quarter **sìfēnzhīyī** 四分之一

quarter of an hour **yíkèzhōng** 一刻钟

queen **wánghòu** 王后

question **wèntí** 问题

queue **páiduì** 排队

quick **kuài** 快

quiet **ānjìng** 安静

quilt **bèizi** 被子

R

rabbit **tùzi** 兔子

radio **shōuyīnjī** 收音机

railway **tiělù** 铁路

railway station **huǒchēzhàn** 火车站

rain **yǔ** 雨

rain (verb) **xiàyǔ** 下雨

raincoat 雨衣 **yǔyī**

rape **qiángjiān** 强奸

rapids **jíliú** 急流

rare **nándé** 难得

rash **zhěnzi** 疹子

rat **hàozi/lǎoshǔ** 耗子／老鼠

raw **shēngde** 生的

razor blade **tìdāopiàn** 剃刀片

read **kànshū** 看书

ready **zhǔnbèihǎole** 准备好了

really **shíjì** 实际

reason **yuányīn** 原因

receipt **shōujù** 收据

receive **shōudào** 收到

reception desk **fúwùtái** 服务台

recommend **tuījiàn** 推荐

rectangle **chángfāngxíng** 长方形

red **hóngsè** 红色

red wine **hóng pútaojiǔ/hóngjiǔ** 红葡萄酒／红酒

reduction **jiàngjià** 降价

refrigerator **bīngxiāng** 冰箱

refund **tuìkuǎn** 退款

refuse **jùjué** 拒绝

regards **wènhòu** 问候

region **dìqū** 地区

registered **guàhào** 挂号

registered mail **guàhào yóujiàn** 挂号邮件

regret **yíhàn** 遗憾

relatives **qīnqi** 亲戚

reliable **kěkào** 可靠

religion 宗教 **zōngjiào**

remember **jìde** 记得

rent/hire **zū** 租

repair **xiū** 修

repeat **chóngfù** 重复

report (police) **bàojǐng** 报警

represent **dàibiǎo** 代表

reserve **bǎoliú** 保留

responsible **fùzé** 负责

rest **xiūxi** 休息

restaurant **fànguǎn** 饭馆

restroom **xǐshǒujiān** 洗手间

result **jiéguǒ** 结果

retired **tuìxiū** 退休

return (come back) **huílái** 回来

return (give back) **huán** 还

return (go back) **huíqù** 回去

return ticket **láihuípiào** 来回票

reverse charges **duìfāng fùfèi** 对方付费

rheumatism **fēngshībìng** 风湿病

ribbon **sīdài** 丝带

rice (cooked) **mǐfàn** 米饭

rice (grain) **dàmǐ** 大米

ridiculous **kěxiàode** 可笑的

riding (horseback) **qímǎ** 骑马

right (correct) **zhèngquè** 正确

right (side) **yòubiān** 右边

right of way **yōuxiān** 优先

ring **jièzhi** 戒指

rinse **chōngxǐ** 冲洗

ripe **shúde** 熟的

risk **màoxiǎn** 冒险

river **hé** 河

road **lù** 路

roadway **chēxíngdào** 车行道

roasted **hōngkǎo** 烘烤

rock (stone) **shítou** 石头

roof **wūdǐng** 屋顶

room **fángjiān** 房间

room number **fángjiān hàomǎ** 房间号码

room service **kèfáng fúwù** 客房服务

rope **shéngzi** 绳子

round **yuánxíngde** 圆形的

route **lùxiàn** 路线

rowing boat **huátǐng** 划艇

rubber (eraser) **xiàngpícā** 橡皮擦

rubber (material) **xiàngjiāo** 橡胶

rude **wúlǐde** 无礼的

ruins **yíjì** 遗迹

run (verb) **pǎo** 跑

running shoes **sàipǎoxié** 赛跑鞋

S

sad **nánguò** 难过

safe **ānquán** 安全

safe (for cash) **bǎoxiǎnxiāng** 保险箱

safety pin **biézhēn** 别针

salad **shālā** 沙拉

sale **chūshòu** 出售

sales clerk **shòuhuòyuán** 售货员

salt **yán** 盐

same **yíyàng** 一样

sandals **liángxié** 凉鞋

sandy beach **shātān** 沙滩

sanitary napkin, sanitary towel **wèishēngjīn** 卫生巾

satisfied **mǎnyì** 满意

Saturday **Xīngqíliù** 星期六

sauce **tiáowèizhī** 调味汁

saucepan **píngdǐguō** 平底锅

sauna **sāngnáyù** 桑拿浴

say **shuō** 说

scald (injury) **tàngshāng** 烫伤

scales **chèng/tiānpíng** 秤／天平

scarf **wéijīn** 围巾

scarf (headscarf) **tóujīn** 头巾

scenery **zìrán fēngjǐng** 自然风景

schedule **shíkèbiǎo/rìchéngbiǎo** 时刻表／日程表

school **xuéxiào** 学校

scissors **jiǎndāo** 剪刀

screwdriver **qǐzi/luósīdāo** 起子／螺丝刀

sculpture **diāosù** 雕塑

sea **hǎi** 海

seafood **hǎixiān** 海鲜

season **jìjié** 季节

seat **zuòwèi** 座位

second (in line) **dì'èr ge** 第二个

second (instant) **miǎo** 秒

sedative **zhènjìngjì** 镇静剂

see **kànjiàn** 看见

seem **sìhū** 似乎

send (fax) **fā** 发

send (post) **jì** 寄

sentence **jùzi** 句子

separate **fēnkāi** 分开

September **Jiǔyuè** 九月

serious **yánsù** 严肃

serious (injury) **yánzhòng** 严重

service **fúwù** 服务

seven **qī** 七

seventeen **shíqī** 十七

seventy **qīshí** 七十

sew **féng** 缝

shade **yīnliángchù** 阴凉处

shallow **qiǎn** 浅

shampoo **xǐfàjì** 洗发剂

shark **shāyú** 鲨鱼

shave (verb) **guā húzi** 刮胡子

shaver **diàndòng tìdāo** 电动剃刀

shaving cream **xiūmiànshuāng** 修面霜

she, her **tā** 她

sheet **bèidān** 被单

shirt **chènshān/chènyī** 衬衫／衬衣

shoe **xié** 鞋

shoe polish **xiéyóu** 鞋油

shop, store **shāngdiàn** 商店

shop (verb) **gòuwù** 购物

shop assistant **yíngyèyuán** 营业员

shop window **chúchuāng** 橱窗

shopping center **gòuwù zhōngxīn** 购物中心

short (height) **ǎi** 矮

short (length) **duǎn** 短

shorts (short trousers) **duǎnkù** 短裤

shoulder **jiānbǎng** 肩膀

show to **gěi...kàn** 给…看

shower (for washing) **línyù** 淋浴

shower (rain) **zhènyǔ** 阵雨

shrimp **xiǎoxiā** 小虾

shuttle bus **jiēbóchē** 接驳车

shy **hàixiū** 害羞

sightseeing **guān'guāng** 观光

sign (road) **lùbiāo** 路标

sign (verb), signature **qiānmíng** 签名

silk **sīchóu** 丝绸

silver **yín** 银

simple 简单 **jiǎndān**

since (until now) **zìcóng** 自从

sing **chànggē** 唱歌

single (only one) **dānyī** 单一

single (unmarried) **dānshēn** 单身

single ticket **dānchéngpiào** 单程票

sir **xiānsheng** 先生

sister (older) **jiějie** 姐姐

sister (younger) **mèimei** 妹妹

sit **zuò** 坐

six **liù** 六

sixteen **shíliù** 十六

sixty **liùshí** 六十

size **dàxiǎo** 大小

size (clothes) **chǐcùn** 尺寸

skiing **huáxuě** 滑雪

skin **pífū** 皮肤

skirt **qúnzi** 裙子

sky **tiānkōng** 天空

sleep **shuìjiào** 睡觉

sleeping car **wòpù** 卧铺

sleeping pills **ānmiányào** 安眠药

sleepy **kùn** 困

sleeve **xiùzi** 袖子

slippers **tuōxié** 拖鞋

slow **màn** 慢

small **xiǎo** 小

small change **língqián** 零钱

smelly **chòuwèi** 臭味

smile **xiào** 笑

smoke (verb) **chōuyān** 抽烟

smoke detector **yānhuǒ zhǐshìqì** 烟火指示器

snack **xiǎochī** 小吃

snake **shé** 蛇

snow **xuě** 雪

snow (verb) **xiàxuě** 下雪

soap **féizào** 肥皂

soap powder **zàofěn** 皂粉

soccer **zúqiú** 足球

soccer match **zúqiúsài** 足球赛

social media **shèjiāo méitǐ** 社交媒体

socialism **shèhuìzhǔyì** 社会主义

socket (electric) **chāzuò** 插座

socks **wàzi** 袜子

soft **ruǎn** 软

soft drink **qìshuǐ** 汽水

soft seat **ruǎnzuò** 软座

soft berth **ruǎnwò** 软卧

software **ruǎnjiàn** 软件

soil **nítǔ** 泥土

sole (of shoe) **xiédǐ** 鞋底

some **yìxiē** 一些

someone **yǒurén** 有人

something **shénme** 什么

sometimes **yǒushí** 有时

somewhere **mǒuchù** 某处

son **érzi** 儿子

song **gē** 歌

soon **bùjiǔ** 不久

sore (painful) **tòng/suāntòng** 痛／酸痛

sore (ulcer) **shāngkǒu** 伤口

sore throat **hóulóngténg** 喉咙疼

sorry **duìbuqǐ/bàoqiàn** 对不起／抱歉

soup **tāng** 汤

sour **suān** 酸

south **nánbian** 南边

souvenir **jìniànpǐn** 纪念品

soy sauce (salty) **xián jiàngyóu** 咸酱油

soy sauce (sweet) **tián jiàngyóu** 甜酱油

space **kōngjiān/dìfang** 空间／地方

speak **jiǎng/shuō** 讲／说

special **tèbié** 特别

specialist (doctor) **zhuānkē yīshēng** 专科医生

specialty (cooking) **hǎocài** 好菜

speed limit **xiàndìngde sùdù** 限定的速度

spell **yòng zìmǔ pīn** 用字母拼

spend money **huāqián** 花钱

spices **xiāngliào** 香料

spicy **jiā xiāngliào de/xīnlà de** 加香料的／辛辣的

spider **zhīzhū** 蜘蛛

spoon **tāngchí/tāng sháo** 汤匙／汤勺

sport **tǐyù yùndòng** 体育运动

sports center **tǐyù zhōngxīn** 体育中心

spouse **pèi'ǒu** 配偶

sprain **niǔshāng** 扭伤

spring (season) **chūntiān** 春天

square (plaza) **guǎngchǎng** 广场

square (shape) **zhèngfāngxíng** 正方形

square meter **píngfāngmǐ** 平方米

stadium **tǐyùchǎng** 体育场

stain **wūdiǎn** 污点

stain remover **qùwūjì** 去污剂

stairs **lóutī** 楼梯

stale **bù xīnxiān** 不新鲜

stamp **yóupiào** 邮票

stand up **zhànqǐlái** 站起来

star **xīngxīng** 星星

start **kāishǐ** 开始

station **zhàn** 站

statue **diāoxiàng** 雕像

stay overnight **liúsù/guòyè** 留宿／过夜

steal **tōu** 偷

steamed **zhēngde** 蒸的

stepfather **jìfù** 继父

stepmother **jìmǔ** 继母

steps **táijiē** 台阶

sterilize **xiāodú** 消毒

sticky tape **jiāodài** 胶带

stockings **cháng tǒng wàzi** 长筒袜子

stomach (abdomen) **dùzi** 肚子

stomach (organ) **wèi** 胃

stomach ache **dùzi tòng** 肚子痛

stools (to sit on) **dèngzi** 凳子

stop (bus) **zhàn** 站

stop (cease) **tíng** 停

stop (halt) **zhànzhù** 站住

stopover **zhōngtú tíngliú** 中途停留

store, shop **shāngdiàn** 商店

storm **fēngbào** 风暴

story (building) **céng/lóu** 层／楼

straight **zhíde** 直的

straight ahead **yìzhí zǒu** 一直走

strange **qíguài** 奇怪

straw (drinking) **xīguǎn** 吸管

street **jiē** 街

street vendor **xiǎofàn** 小贩

strike (work stoppage) **bàgōng** 罢工

string **shéngzi** 绳子

strong **qiángzhuàng** 强壮

study (room) **shūfáng** 书房

study (verb) **xué/xuéxí** 学／学习

stupid **bèn/chǔn** 笨／蠢

sturdy **jiēshi** 结实

subtitles **zìmù** 字幕

suburb **jiāoqū** 郊区

subway **dìtiě** 地铁

succeed **chénggōng** 成功

sugar **táng** 糖

suit **yí tào xīfú** 一套西服

suitcase **xiāngzi** 箱子

suite **tàofáng** 套房

summer **xiàtiān** 夏天

sun **tàiyáng** 太阳

Sunday **Xīngqítiān/Xīngqírì** 星期天／星期日

sunglasses **mòjìng** 墨镜

sunrise **rìchū** 日出

sunscreen **fángshàiyóu** 防晒油

sunset **rìluò** 日落

sunshade **yángsǎn** 阳伞

supermarket **chāojí shìchǎng** 超级市场

sure **yídìng** 一定

surface mail **hǎi/lù yóujì** 海／陆邮寄

surname **xìng** 姓

surprise **jīngqí** 惊奇

swallow (verb) **tūn** 吞

swamp **zhǎozédì** 沼泽地

sweat (verb) **chūhàn** 出汗

sweater **máoyī** 毛衣

sweet **tián** 甜

swim (verb) **yóuyǒng** 游泳

swimming costume **yóuyǒngyī** 游泳衣

swimming pool **yóuyǒngchí** 游泳池

switch (light) **diàndēng kāiguān** 电灯开关

swollen **zhǒngle** 肿了

syrup **tángjiāng** 糖浆

T

table **zhuōzi** 桌子

table tennis **pīngpāngqiú** 乒乓球

tablecloth **zhuōbù** 桌布

tablemat **diànzi** 垫子

tablespoon **dà tāngchí** 大汤匙

tablets **yàopiàn** 药片

tableware **cānjù** 餐具

tailor's **cáiféng diàn** 裁缝店

take (medicine) **chīyào** 吃药

take (photograph) **zhàoxiàng** 照相

take (time) **xūyào (shíjiān)** 需要(时间)

takeaway **dàizǒu** 带走

talk **tánhuà** 谈话

tall **gāo** 高

tampon **wèishēng miántiáo** 卫生棉条

Taoism **Dàojiào** 道教

tap **shuǐlóngtóu** 水龙头

tap water **fēi yǐnyòngshuǐ** 非饮用水

tape measure **ruǎnchǐ** 软尺

tape recorder **lùyīnjī** 录音机

taste (flavor) **wèidào** 味道

taste (style) **qùwèi** 趣味

taste (verb) **cháng** 尝

tasty **hǎochī** 好吃

tax **shuì** 税

tax-free shop **miǎnshuì diàn** 免税店

taxi **chūzū qìchē** 出租汽车

taxi stand **chūzū qìchēzhàn** 出租汽车站

tea (black) 红茶 **hóng chá**

tea (green) **lǜchá** 绿茶

tea house **chálóu** 茶楼

teacup **chábēi** 茶杯

teapot **cháhú** 茶壶

teaspoon **chásháo** 茶勺

teat (bottle) **xiàngpí nǎitóu** 橡皮奶头

telephoto lens **wàngyuǎn jìngtóu** 望远镜头

television **diànshì** 电视

tell **gàosu** 告诉

temperature (body) **tǐwēn** 体温

temperature (heat) **wēndù** 温度

temple **sìyuàn** 寺院

temporary **zànshí** 暂时

tender, sore **cuìruòde** 脆弱的

tennis **wǎngqiú** 网球

tennis court **wǎngqiúchǎng** 网球场

ten **shí** 十

ten thousand **wàn** 万

tent **zhàngpeng** 帐篷

terminal **hángzhàn** 航站

terminus **zhōngdiǎnzhàn** 终点站

thank **gǎnxiè** 感谢

thank you, thanks **xièxie** 谢谢

that **nà (ge)** 那(个)

thaw (verb) **jiědòng** 解冻

theater **jùyuàn** 剧院

theft **tōudào** 偷盗

their **tāmende** 他们的

there **nàbiān** 那边

there is (are) **yǒu** 有

thermometer (body) **tǐwēnjì** 体温计

thermometer (weather) **wēndùjì** 温度计

they **tāmen** 他们

thick **hòu** 厚

thief **zéi** 贼

thigh **dàtuǐ** 大腿

thin (not fat) **shòu** 瘦

thin (not thick) **bó** 薄

thing **dōngxi** 东西

think (believe) **xiāngxìn** 相信

think (ponder) **xiǎng/kǎolǜ** 想／考虑

third (in a series) **dìsān** 第三

third (1/3) **sānfēnzhīyī** 三分之一

thirsty **kě** 渴

this **zhè (ge)** 这(个)

this afternoon **jīntiān xiàwǔ** 今天下午

this evening **jīntiān wǎnshàng** 今天晚上

this morning **jīntiān zǎoshang** 今天早上

thousand **qiān** 千

thread **xiàn** 线

three **sān** 三

throat **hóulóng** 喉咙

throat lozenges **rùnhóutáng** 润喉糖

through (passage) **jīngguò** 经过

thunder (verb) **dǎléi** 打雷

thunderstorm **léibàoyǔ** 雷暴雨

Thursday **Xīngqísì** 星期四

ticket (admission) **rùchǎngquàn** 入场券

ticket (travel) **piào** 票

ticket office **shòupiàochù** 售票处

tide **cháoshuǐ** 潮水

tidy **zhěngqí** 整齐

tie (necktie) **lǐngdài** 领带

tie (verb) **jì** 系

tights (pantyhose) **kùwà** 裤袜

tights (thick) **jǐnshēn yīkù** 紧身衣裤

time **shíjiān** 时间

time (occasion) **cì** 次

times (multiplying) **chéng** 乘

timetable **shíkèbiǎo** 时刻表

tin (can) **guàntou** 罐头

tin opener **guàntoudāo** 罐头刀

tip (gratuity) **xiǎofèi** 小费

tire **lúntāi** 轮胎

tired **lèi** 累

tissues (facial) **zhǐjīn** 纸巾

toast (bread) **kǎo miànbāo** 烤面包

toast (with drinks) **gānbēi** 干杯

tobacco **yāncǎo** 烟草

today **jīntiān** 今天

toddler **yòu'ér** 幼儿

toe **jiǎozhǐ** 脚趾

together **yìqǐ** 一起

toilet **cèsuǒ/xǐshǒujiān** 厕所／洗手间

toilet (seated) **zuòcè** 坐厕

toilet (squat) **dūncè** 蹲厕

toilet bowl **chōushuǐ mǎtǒng** 抽水马桶

toilet paper **wèishēngzhǐ** 卫生纸

toilet seat **mǎtǒng zuòquān** 马桶座圈

toiletries **shūzhuāng yòngpǐn** 梳妆用品

tomato **xīhóngshì** 西红柿

tomb **língmù** 陵墓

tomorrow **míngtiān** 明天

tongue **shétou** 舌头

tonight **jīnwǎn** 今晚

too **tài** 太

tool **gōngjù** 工具

tooth **yá** 牙

toothache **yáténg** 牙疼

toothbrush **yáshuā** 牙刷

toothpaste **yágāo** 牙膏

toothpick **yáqiān** 牙签

top **dǐng** 顶

top up **jiāmǎn** 加满

torch, flashlight **shǒudiàntǒng** 手电筒

total **yígòng** 一共

touch **mō** 摸

tour **cānguān** 参观

tour group **lǚxíngtuán** 旅行团

tour guide **dǎoyóu** 导游

tourist class **jīngjìcāng** 经济舱

toward **xiàng** 向

towel **máojīn** 毛巾

tower **tǎ** 塔

town **shìzhèn** 市镇

toy **wánjù** 玩具

trade **màoyì** 贸易

traffic **jiāotōng** 交通

traffic light **hónglǜdēng** 红绿灯

train **huǒchē** 火车

train station **huǒchēzhàn** 火车站

train ticket **huǒchēpiào** 火车票

train timetable **huǒchē shíkèbiǎo** 火车时刻表

transfer (bank) **guòhù** 过户

translate (verb) **fānyì/bǐyì** 翻译／笔译

translator **fānyìzhě** 翻译者

travel **lǚxíng** 旅行

travel agent **lǚxíngshè** 旅行社

traveler **lǚyóuzhě/lǚkè** 旅游者／旅客

traveler's check **lǚxíng zhīpiào** 旅行支票

traveling bag **lǚxíngbāo** 旅行包

treatment **zhìliáo** 治疗

tree **shù** 树

triangle **sānjiǎoxíng** 三角形

trim (haircut) **xiūjiǎn** 修剪

trip (travel) **lǚxíng/lǚchéng** 旅行／旅程

trouble **máfan** 麻烦

trousers **kùzi** 裤子

truck **kǎchē** 卡车

true **zhēnde** 真的

trustworthy **kěxìnde** 可信的

try **shì** 试

try on **shìchuān** 试穿

Tuesday **Xīngqí'èr** 星期二

tunnel **suìdào** 隧道

turn (change direction) **zhuǎn** 转

turn off **guānshang** 关上

turn on **kāi** 开

TV **diànshì** 电视

TV guide **diànshì zhǐnán**
电视指南

tweezers **nièzi** 镊子

twelve **shí'èr** 十二

twice **liǎng cì** 两次

Twitter **tuītè** 推特

two (measure) **liǎng** 两

two (numeral) **èr** 二

typhoon **táifēng** 台风

U

ugly **nánkàn/chǒu** 难看／丑

ulcer **kuìyáng** 溃疡

umbrella **sǎn** 伞

under **zài...dǐxia** 在…底下

underground (subway) **dìtiě**
地铁

underpants **nèikù** 内裤

understand **dǒng** 懂

underwear **nèiyī** 内衣

undress **tuō yīfú** 脱衣服

unemployed **shīyè** 失业

uneven **bù píngtǎn** 不平坦

university **dàxué** 大学

unleaded petrol **wúqiān qìyóu**
无铅汽油

until **zhídào** 直到

up **shàng** 上

upset (unhappy) **fánmèn** 烦闷

upset stomach **wèi bù shūfú**
胃不舒服

upstairs **lóushàng** 楼上

urgent **jǐnjí** 紧急

urine **niào** 尿

urinate (verb) **xiǎobiàn** 小便

us **wǒmen** 我们

use **yòng** 用

used up **yòngwánle** 用完了

useful **yǒuyòngde** 有用的

useless **wúyòngde** 无用的

usually **tōngcháng** 通常

V

vacancy **kōngfáng** 空房

vacant **kōngde** 空的

vacation **jiàqī** 假期

vacuum flask **bǎowēnpíng**
保温瓶

vagina **yīndào** 阴道

valid **yǒuxiào** 有效

valley **shāngǔ** 山谷

valuable **guìzhòng** 贵重

valuables **guìzhòng wùpǐn**
贵重物品

value **jiàzhí** 价值

van **bānyùnchē** 搬运车

vase **huāpíng** 花瓶

vegetable **shūcài** 蔬菜

vegetarian **chīsùde** 吃素的

vein **xuèguǎn/jìngmài** 血管／
静脉

velvet **tiān'éróng** 天鹅绒

vending machine **zìdòng
shòuhuòjī** 自动售货机

venereal disease **xìngbìng** 性病

venomous **yǒudúde** 有毒的

vertical **chuízhíde** 垂直的

very **hěn** 很

via **jīngyóu** 经由

vicinity **fùjìn** 附近

video camera **shèxiàngjī** 摄像机

view **fēngjǐng** 风景

village **cūnzhuāng** 村庄

vinegar **cù** 醋

visa **qiānzhèng** 签证

visit **fǎngwèn** 访问

visiting time **cānguān shíjiān**
参观时间

vitamin tablets **wéishēngsùpiàn** 维生素片

vitamins **wéishēngsù** 维生素

volleyball **páiqiú** 排球

vomit **ǒutù** 呕吐

vulgar **cūsúde** 粗俗的

W

wage **gōngzī** 工资

waist **yāo** 腰

wait **děng** 等

waiter **nánfúwùyuán** 男服务员

waiting room **hòuchēshì** 候车室

waitress **nǚfúwùyuán** 女服务员

wake **jiàoxǐng** 叫醒

wake up **xǐng lái** 醒来

walk (noun) **sànbù** 散步

walk (verb) **zǒu** 走

walking stick **guǎizhàng** 拐杖

wall **qiáng** 墙

wallet **qiánbāo** 钱包

want **yào** 要

war **zhànzhēng** 战争

warm **wēnnuǎnde** 温暖的

warn (verb), warning **jǐnggào** 警告

wash **xǐ** 洗

washing (noun) **yào xǐ de yīfu** 要洗的衣服

washing machine **xǐyījī** 洗衣机

washing powder **xǐyīfěn** 洗衣粉

washing room **xǐshǒujiān** 洗手间

watch (look after) **kānguǎn** 看管

watch (wristwatch) **biǎo** 表

watch out **xiǎoxīn** 小心

water **shuǐ** 水

waterfall **pùbù** 瀑布

watermelon **xīguā** 西瓜

waterproof **bútòushuǐde** 不透水的

way (direction) **fāngxiàng** 方向

way (method) **fāngfǎ** 方法

we **wǒmen** 我们

weak **ruò** 弱

wealthy **yǒuqián/fùyǒude** 有钱／富有的

wear (clothing) **chuān** 穿

weather **tiānqì** 天气

weather forecast **tiānqì yùbào** 天气预报

wedding **hūnlǐ** 婚礼

Wednesday **Xīngqísān** 星期三

week **xīngqí** 星期

weekday **gōngzuòrì** 工作日

weekend **zhōumò** 周末

weigh (verb) **chēng** 称

weigh out **chēngchū** 称出

weight **zhòngliàng** 重量

welcome **huānyíng** 欢迎

well (good) **hǎo** 好

well (for water) **jǐng** 井

west **xībiān** 西边

West (Occident) **Xīfāng** 西方

Western style **Xīshì** 西式

Westernized **Xīhuàde** 西化的

wet **shīde** 湿的

what **shénme** 什么

wheelchair **lúnyǐ** 轮椅

when **shénme shíhou** 什么时候

where **nǎli/nǎr** 哪里／哪儿

which **nǎ ge** 哪个

wide **kuān** 宽

white **báisè** 白色

white wine **bái pútaojiǔ** 白葡萄酒

who **shéi/shuí** 谁

whose **shéide/shuíde** 谁的

whole **quánbù/zhěngge** 全部／
整个

why **wèishéme** 为什么

wide-angle lens **guǎngjiǎojìng**
广角镜

widow **guǎfù** 寡妇

widower **guānfū** 鳏夫

wife **qīzi** 妻子

wildlife **yěshēng dòngwù**
野生动物

willing **yuànyì** 愿意

win **yíng** 赢

wind **fēng** 风

window (in room) **chuānghu**
窗户

windscreen, windshield
dǎngfēng bōli 挡风玻璃

windshield wiper **yǔshuā** 雨刷

wine **pútaojiǔ** 葡萄酒

winter **dōngtiān** 冬天

wire **jīnshǔxiàn** 金属线

wish **xīwàng** 希望

withdraw (bank) **tíkuǎn** 提款

without **méiyǒu** 没有

witness **zhèngrén** 证人

woman **nǚrén** 女人

wonderful **hǎojíle** 好极了

wood **mùtou** 木头

wool (knitting) **máoxiàn** 毛线

wool (material) **yángmáo** 羊毛

word **cí** 词

work **gōngzuò** 工作

working day **gōngzuò tiān**
工作天

world **shìjiè** 世界

worried **dānxīn** 担心

worse **gènghuàide/gèng chàde**
更坏的／更差的

worst **zuìhuài de/zuìchà de**
最坏的／最差的

worthwhile **zhíde** 值得

wound **shāngkǒu** 伤口

wrap **bāo** 包

wrapping (paper) **bāozhuāngzhǐ**
包装纸

wrench, spanner **bānshǒu** 扳手

wrist **shǒuwàn** 手腕

wristwatch **biǎo** 表

write **xiě** 写

write down **xiěxiàlái** 写下来

writer **zuòjiā** 作家

writing pad **xiězìběn** 写字本

wrong **cuòde** 错的

X

x-ray **X guāng piànzi** X光片子

Y

year **nián** 年

yellow **huángsè** 黄色

yes **duì** 对

yes, please (acceptance) **hǎo a**
好啊

yesterday **zuótiān** 昨天

you **nǐ** 你

you (plural) **nǐmen** 你们

you're welcome **búxiè** 不谢

young **niánqīng** 年轻

youth hostel **qīngnián**
zhāodàisuǒ 青年招待所

Z

zero **líng** 零

zip **lāliàn** 拉链

zip (verb) **kòushàng lāliàn**
扣上拉链

zoo **dòngwùyuán** 动物园

ABOUT TUTTLE
"Books to Span the East and West"

Our core mission at Tuttle Publishing is to create books which bring people together one page at a time. Tuttle was founded in 1832 in the small New England town of Rutland, Vermont (USA). Our fundamental values remain as strong today as they were then—to publish best-in-class books informing the English-speaking world about the countries and peoples of Asia. The world has become a smaller place today and Asia's economic, cultural and political influence has expanded, yet the need for meaningful dialogue and information about this diverse region has never been greater. Since 1948, Tuttle has been a leader in publishing books on the cultures, arts, cuisines, languages and literatures of Asia. Our authors and photographers have won numerous awards and Tuttle has published thousands of books on subjects ranging from martial arts to paper crafts. We welcome you to explore the wealth of information available on Asia at www.tuttlepublishing.com.

Published by Tuttle Publishing, an imprint of Periplus Editions (HK) Ltd.

www.tuttlepublishing.com

Copyright © 2017 Periplus Editions

Library of Congress Control Number: 2017942021

ISBN 978-0-8048-4685-1

23 22 21 20 19 18 17
10 9 8 7 6 5 4 3 2 1   1707MP

Printed in Singapore

TUTTLE PUBLISHING® is a registered trademark of Tuttle Publishing, a division of Periplus Editions (HK) Ltd.

Distributed by

North America, Latin America & Europe
Tuttle Publishing
364 Innovation Drive
North Clarendon, VT 05759-9436 U.S.A.
Tel: 1 (802) 773-8930
Fax: 1 (802) 773-6993
info@tuttlepublishing.com
www.tuttlepublishing.com

Japan
Tuttle Publishing
Yaekari Building 3rd Floor 5-4-12 Osaki
Shinagawa-ku, Tokyo 141 0032
Tel: (81) 3 5437-0171
Fax: (81) 3 5437-0755
sales@tuttle.co.jp
www.tuttle.co.jp

Asia Pacific
Berkeley Books Pte. Ltd.
61 Tai Seng Avenue #02-12
Singapore 534167
Tel: (65) 6280-1330
Fax: (65) 6280-6290
inquiries@periplus.com.sg
www.periplus.com